D0518005

降击神通
AVATAR
THE LAST AIRBENDER™

Created by
Bryan Konietzko
Michael Dante DiMartino

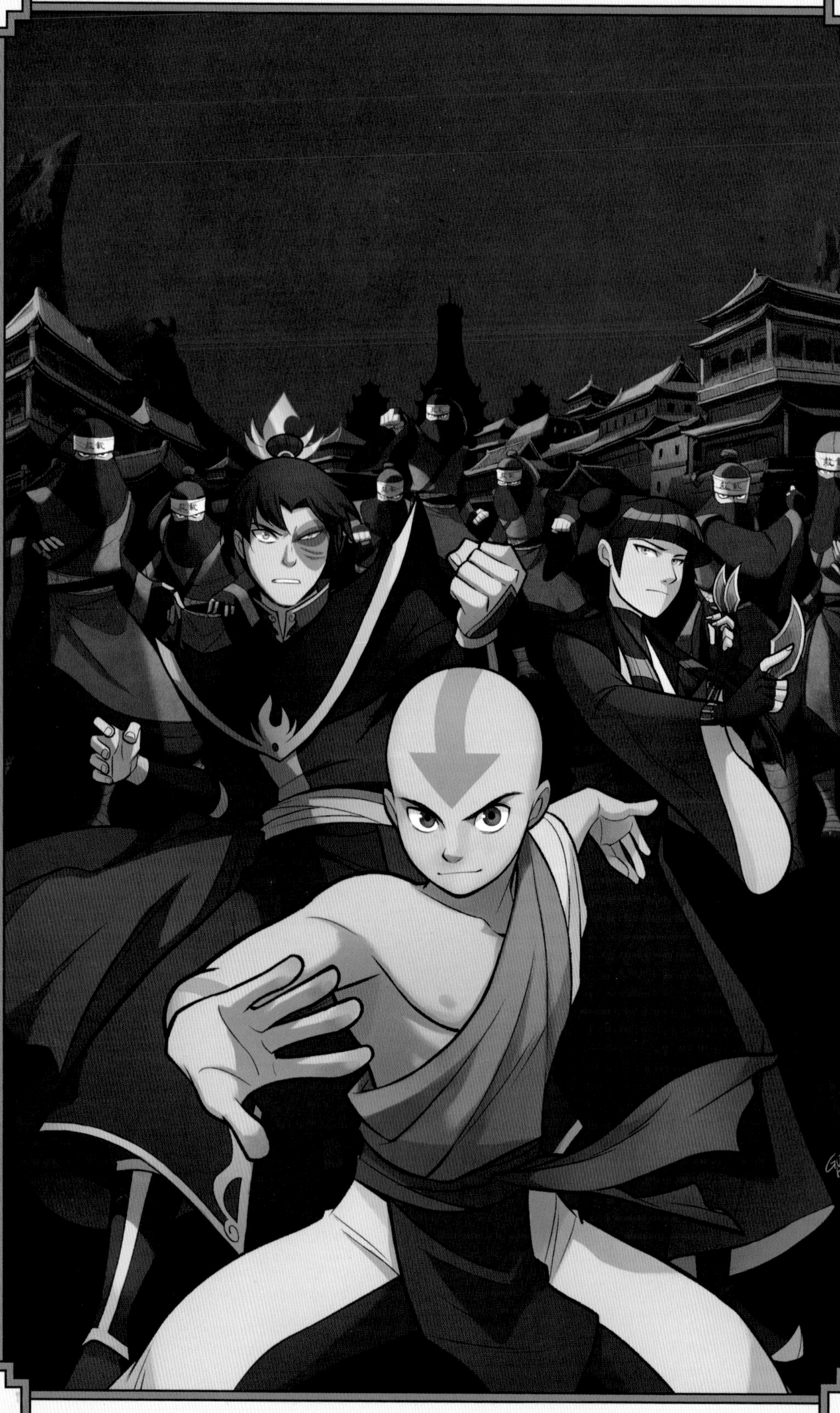

nickelodeon

降击神通

AVATAR

THE LAST AIRBENDER

SMOKE AND SHADOW · PART TWO

script
GENE LUEN YANG

art and cover
GURIHIRU

lettering
MICHAEL HEISLER

DARK HORSE BOOKS

president and publisher
MIKE RICHARDSON

editor
DAVE MARSHALL

associate editor
AARON WALKER

collection designer
ETHAN KIMBERLING

digital art technician
CHRISTIANNE GOUDREAU

Special thanks to Linda Lee, Kat van Dam, James Salerno, and Joan Hilty
at Nickelodeon, and to Bryan Konietzko and Michael Dante DiMartino.

Published by **Dark Horse Books**
A division of Dark Horse Comics LLC
10956 SE Main Street, Milwaukie, OR 97222

DarkHorse.com
Nick.com

International Licensing: (503) 905-2377
To find a comic shop in your area, visit comicshoplocator.com

First edition: December 2015 | ISBN 978-1-61655-790-4

3 5 7 9 10 8 6 4 2
Printed in China

Neil Hankerson, Executive Vice President • Tom Weddle, Chief Financial Officer • Randy Stradley, Vice President of Publishing • Michael Martens, Vice President of Book Trade Sales • Scott Allie, Editor in Chief • Matt Parkinson, Vice President of Marketing • David Scroggy, Vice President of Product Development • Dale LaFountain, Vice President of Information Technology • Ken Lizzi, General Counsel • Davey Estrada, Editorial Director • Chris Warner, Senior Books Editor • Cary Grazzini, Director of Print and Development • Lia Ribacchi, Art Director • Cara Niece, Director of Scheduling • Mark Bernardi, Director of Digital Publishing

Nickelodeon Avatar: The Last Airbender™— Smoke and Shadow Part 2
© 2015 Viacom International, Inc. All rights reserved. Nickelodeon, Nickelodeon Avatar: The Last Airbender, and all related titles, logos, and characters are trademarks of Viacom International, Inc. All other material, unless otherwise specified, is © 2015 Dark Horse Comics LLC. Dark Horse Books® and the Dark Horse logo are registered trademarks of Dark Horse Comics LLC. All rights reserved. No portion of this publication may be reproduced or transmitted, in any form or by any means, without the express written permission of Dark Horse Comics LLC. Names, characters, places, and incidents featured in this publication either are the product of the author's imagination or are used fictitiously. Any resemblance to actual persons (living or dead), events, institutions, or locales, without satiric intent, is coincidental.

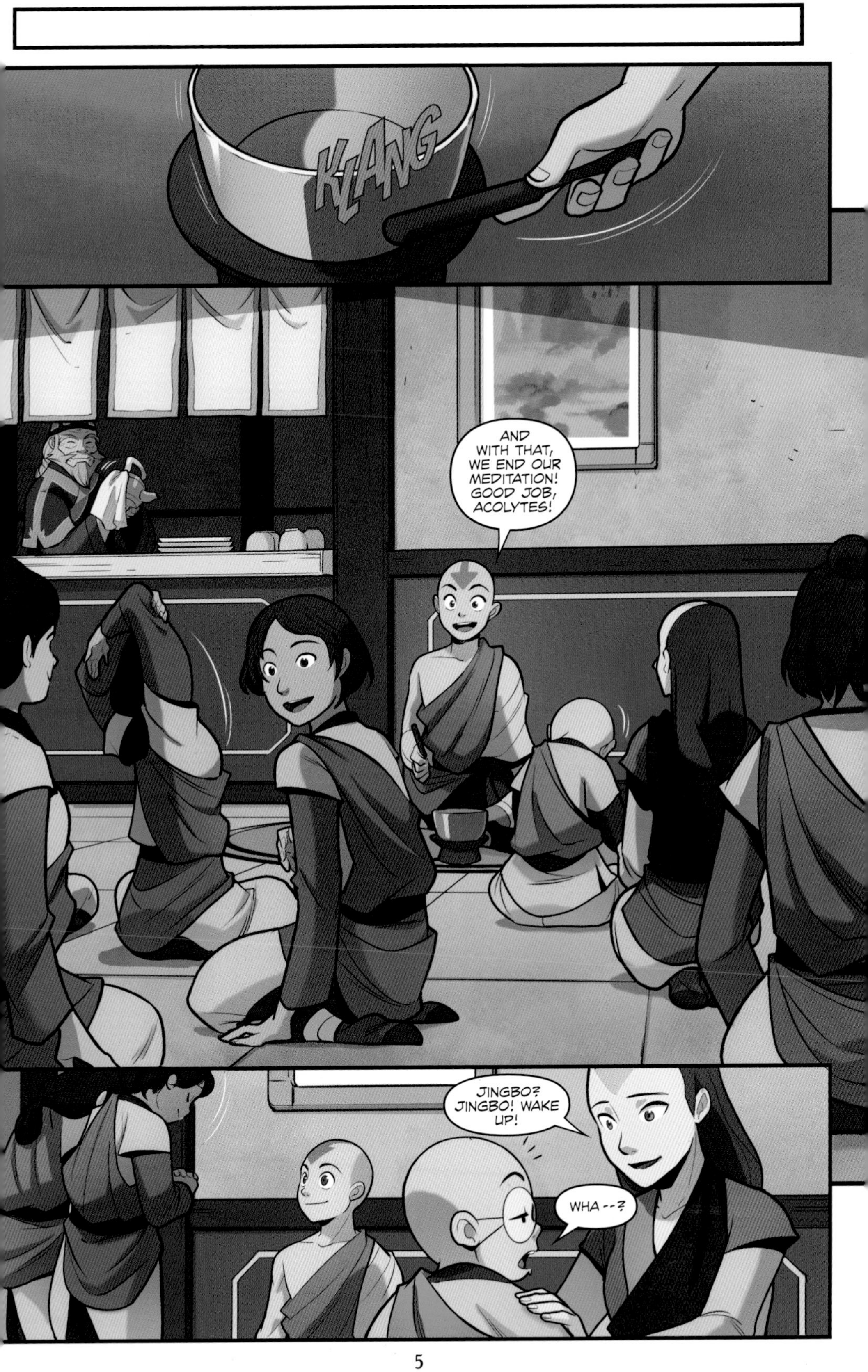
KLANG
AND WITH THAT, WE END OUR MEDITATION! GOOD JOB, ACOLYTES!
JINGBO? JINGBO! WAKE UP!
WHA--?

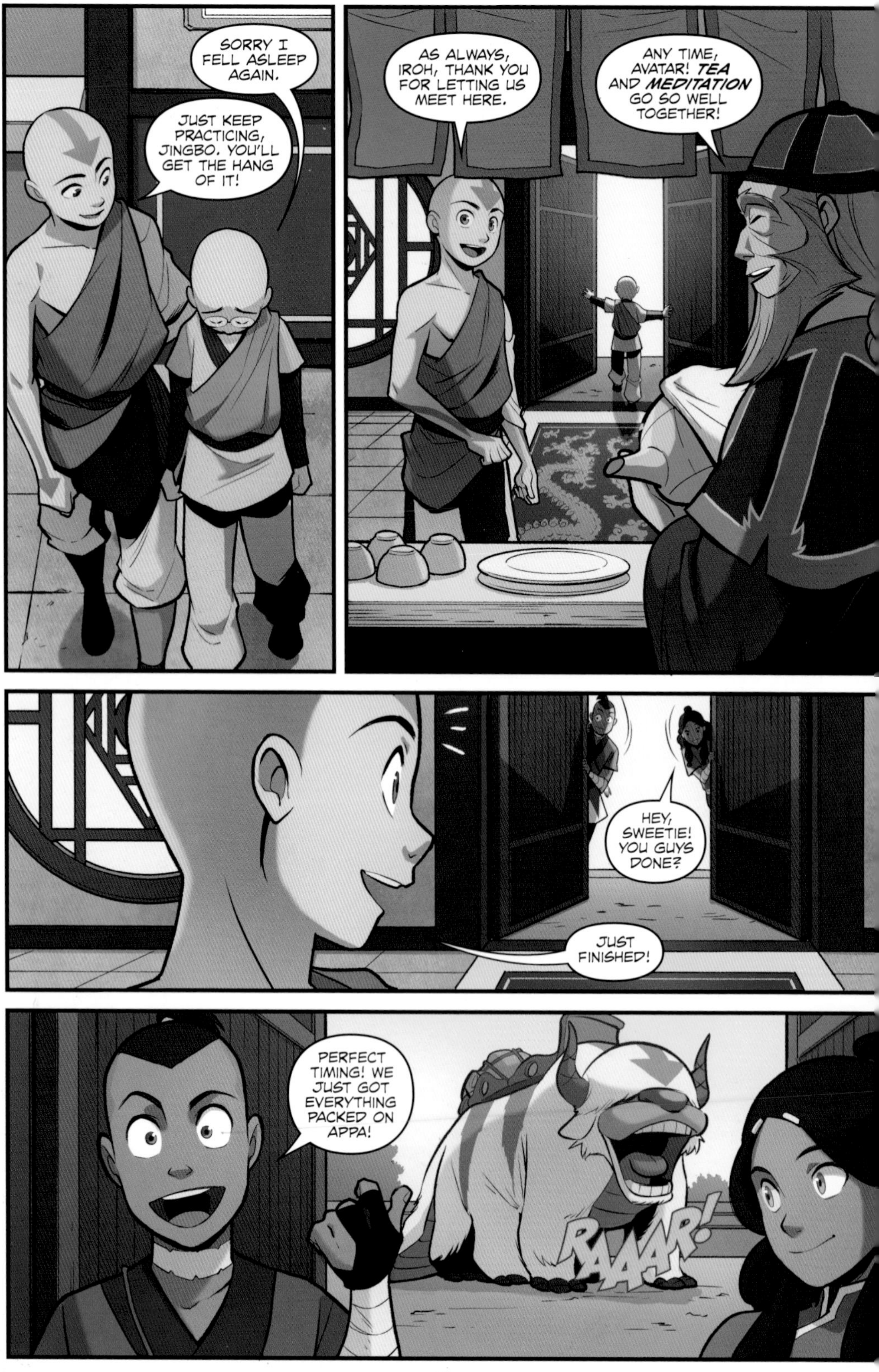
SORRY I FELL ASLEEP AGAIN.
JUST KEEP PRACTICING, JINGBO. YOU'LL GET THE HANG OF IT!
AS ALWAYS, IROH, THANK YOU FOR LETTING US MEET HERE.
ANY TIME, AVATAR! TEA AND MEDITATION GO SO WELL TOGETHER!
HEY, SWEETIE! YOU GUYS DONE?
JUST FINISHED!
PERFECT TIMING! WE JUST GOT EVERYTHING PACKED ON APPA!
RAAAR!

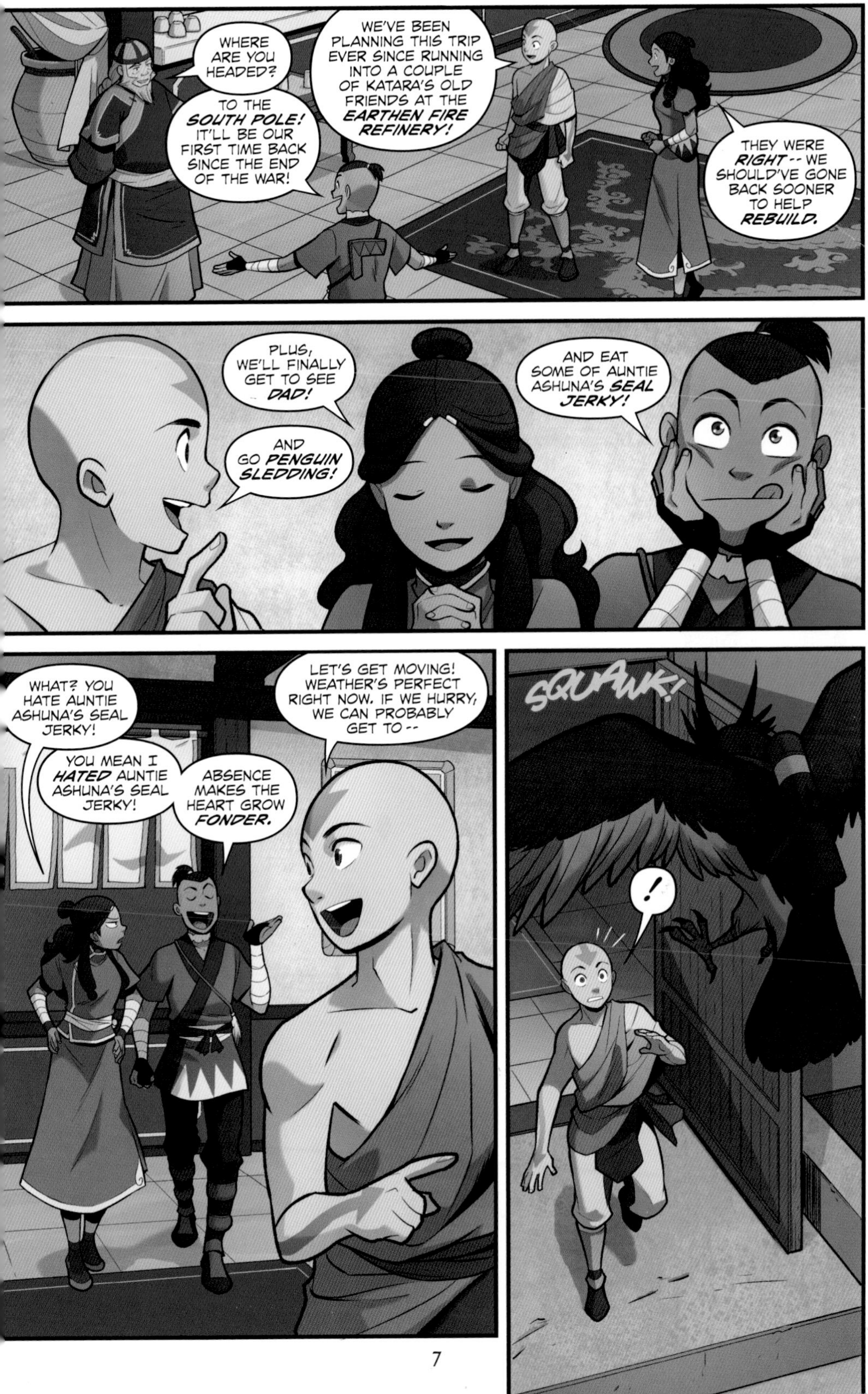

WHERE ARE YOU HEADED?
TO THE SOUTH POLE! IT'LL BE OUR FIRST TIME BACK SINCE THE END OF THE WAR!
WE'VE BEEN PLANNING THIS TRIP EVER SINCE RUNNING INTO A COUPLE OF KATARA'S OLD FRIENDS AT THE EARTHEN FIRE REFINERY!
THEY WERE RIGHT -- WE SHOULD'VE GONE BACK SOONER TO HELP REBUILD.
PLUS, WE'LL FINALLY GET TO SEE DAD!
AND GO PENGUIN SLEDDING!
AND EAT SOME OF AUNTIE ASHUNA'S SEAL JERKY!
WHAT? YOU HATE AUNTIE ASHUNA'S SEAL JERKY!
YOU MEAN I HATED AUNTIE ASHUNA'S SEAL JERKY!
ABSENCE MAKES THE HEART GROW FONDER.
LET'S GET MOVING! WEATHER'S PERFECT RIGHT NOW. IF WE HURRY, WE CAN PROBABLY GET TO --
SQUAWK!
!

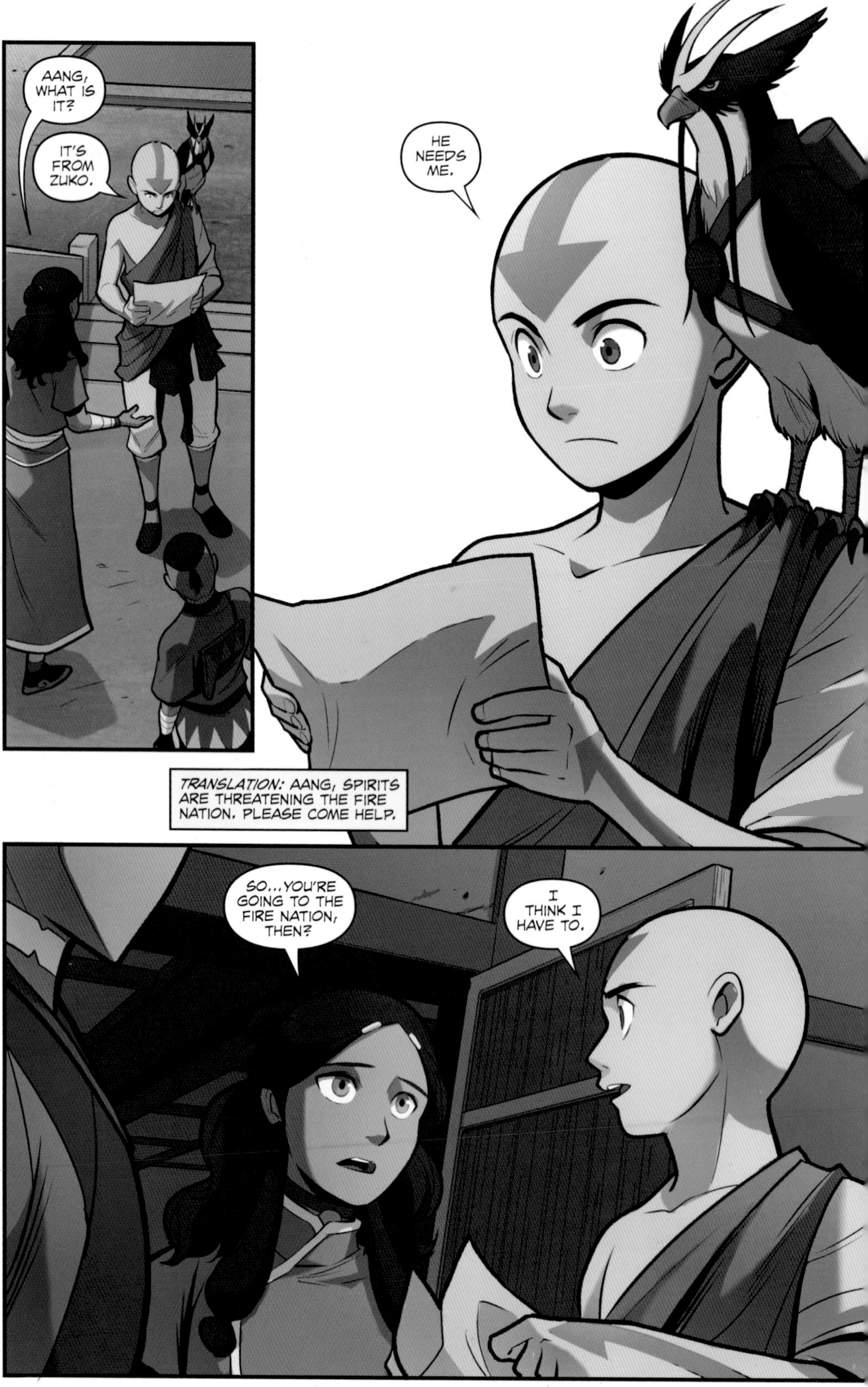
AANG, WHAT IS IT?
IT'S FROM ZUKO.
HE NEEDS ME.
TRANSLATION: AANG, SPIRITS ARE THREATENING THE FIRE NATION. PLEASE COME HELP.
SO...YOU'RE GOING TO THE FIRE NATION, THEN?
I THINK I HAVE TO.

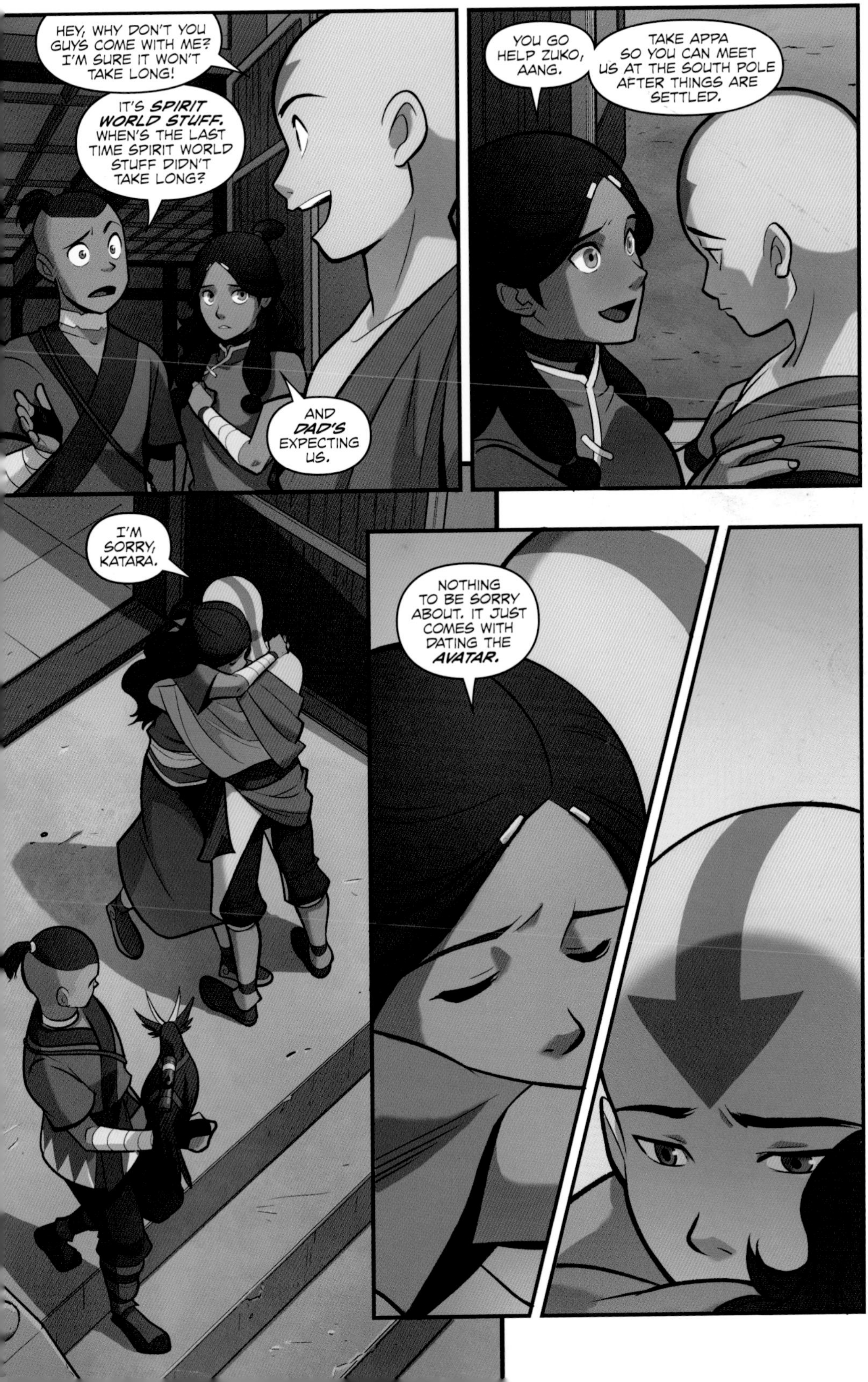
HEY, WHY DON'T YOU GUYS COME WITH ME? I'M SURE IT WON'T TAKE LONG!
IT'S SPIRIT WORLD STUFF. WHEN'S THE LAST TIME SPIRIT WORLD STUFF DIDN'T TAKE LONG?
AND DAD'S EXPECTING US.
YOU GO HELP ZUKO, AANG.
TAKE APPA SO YOU CAN MEET US AT THE SOUTH POLE AFTER THINGS ARE SETTLED.
I'M SORRY, KATARA.
NOTHING TO BE SORRY ABOUT. IT JUST COMES WITH DATING THE AVATAR.

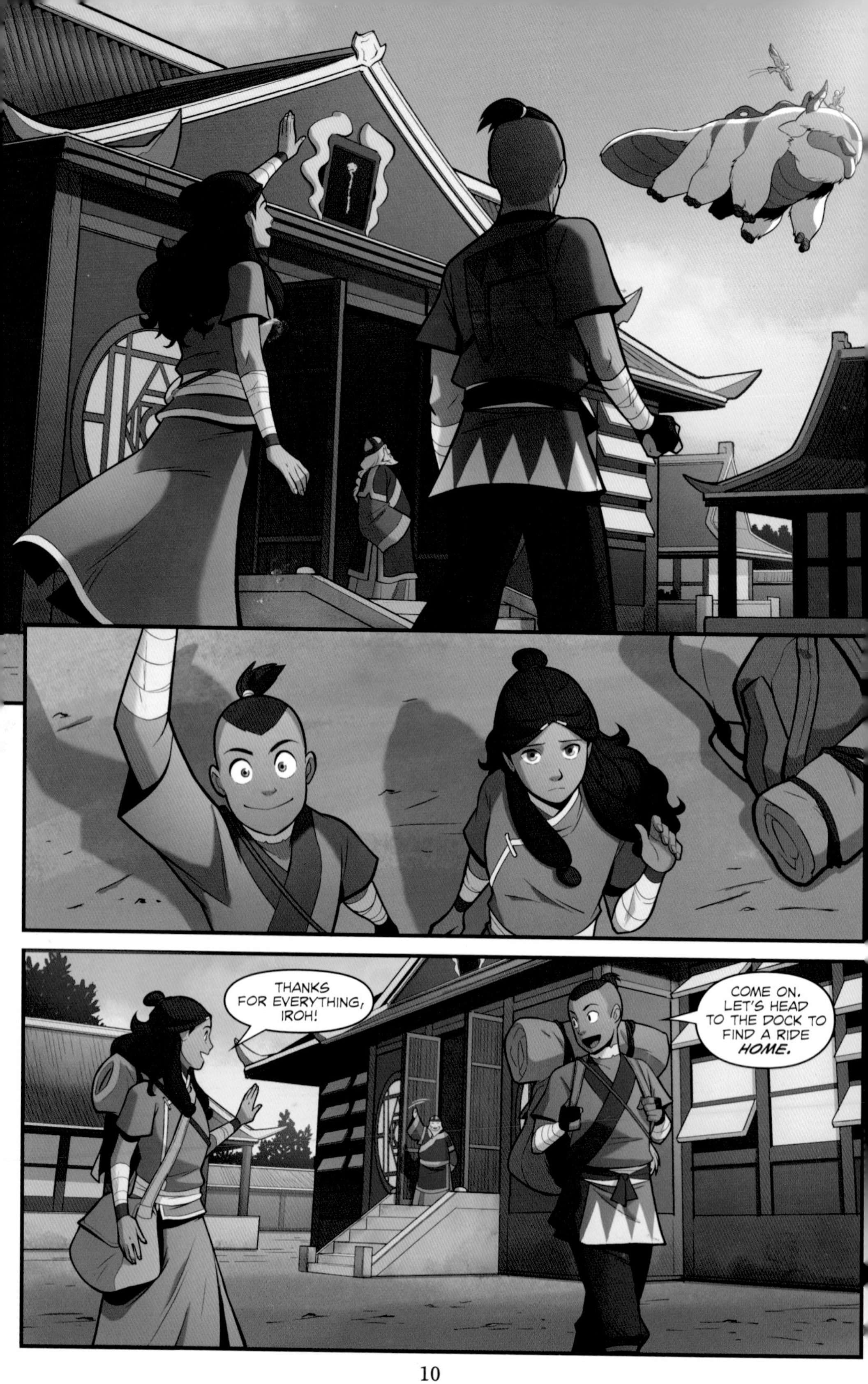
THANKS FOR EVERYTHING, IROH!
COME ON. LET'S HEAD TO THE DOCK TO FIND A RIDE *HOME.*

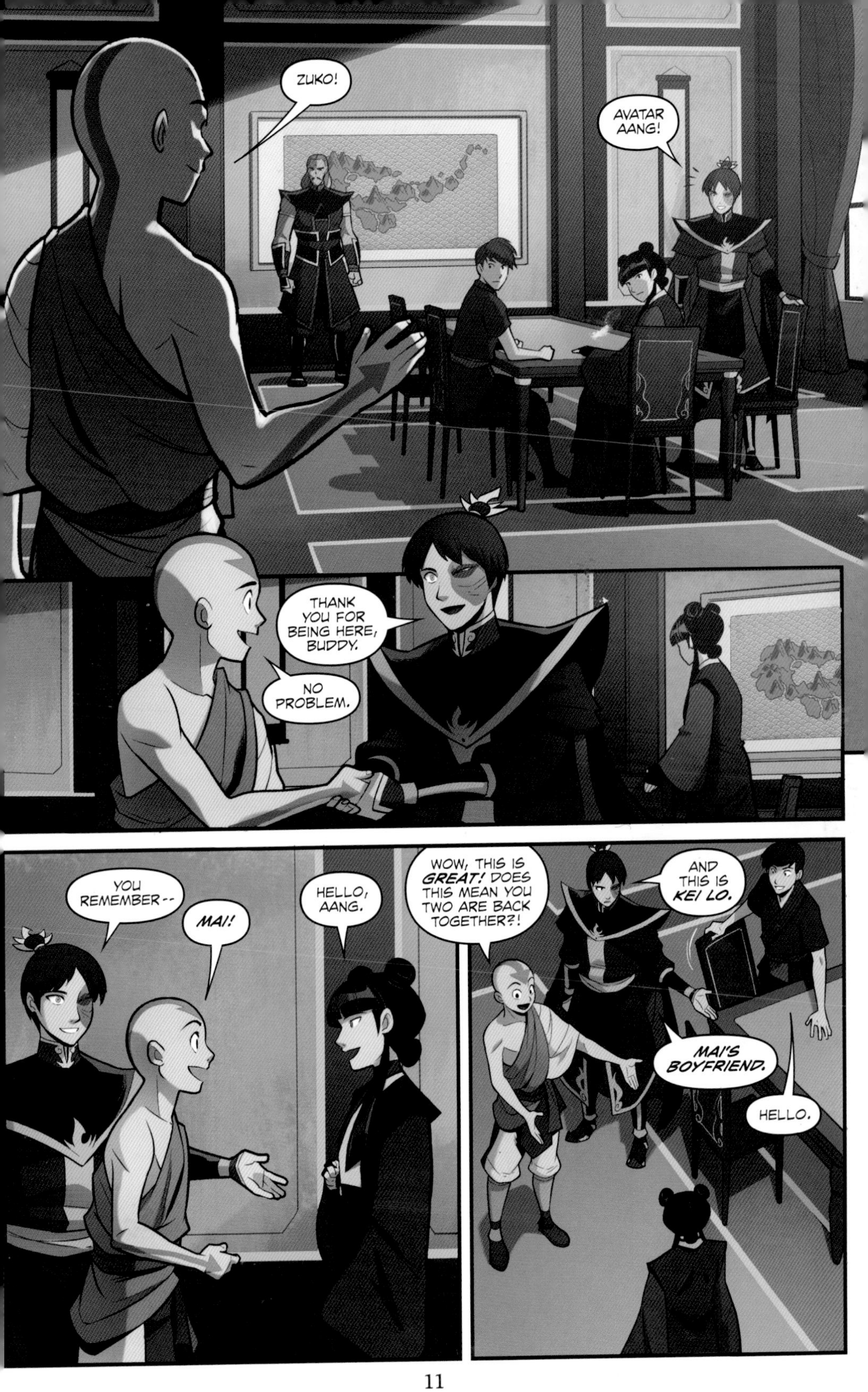
ZUKO!
AVATAR AANG!
THANK YOU FOR BEING HERE, BUDDY.
NO PROBLEM.
YOU REMEMBER--
MAI!
HELLO, AANG.
WOW, THIS IS GREAT! DOES THIS MEAN YOU TWO ARE BACK TOGETHER?!
AND THIS IS KEI LO.
MAI'S BOYFRIEND.
HELLO.

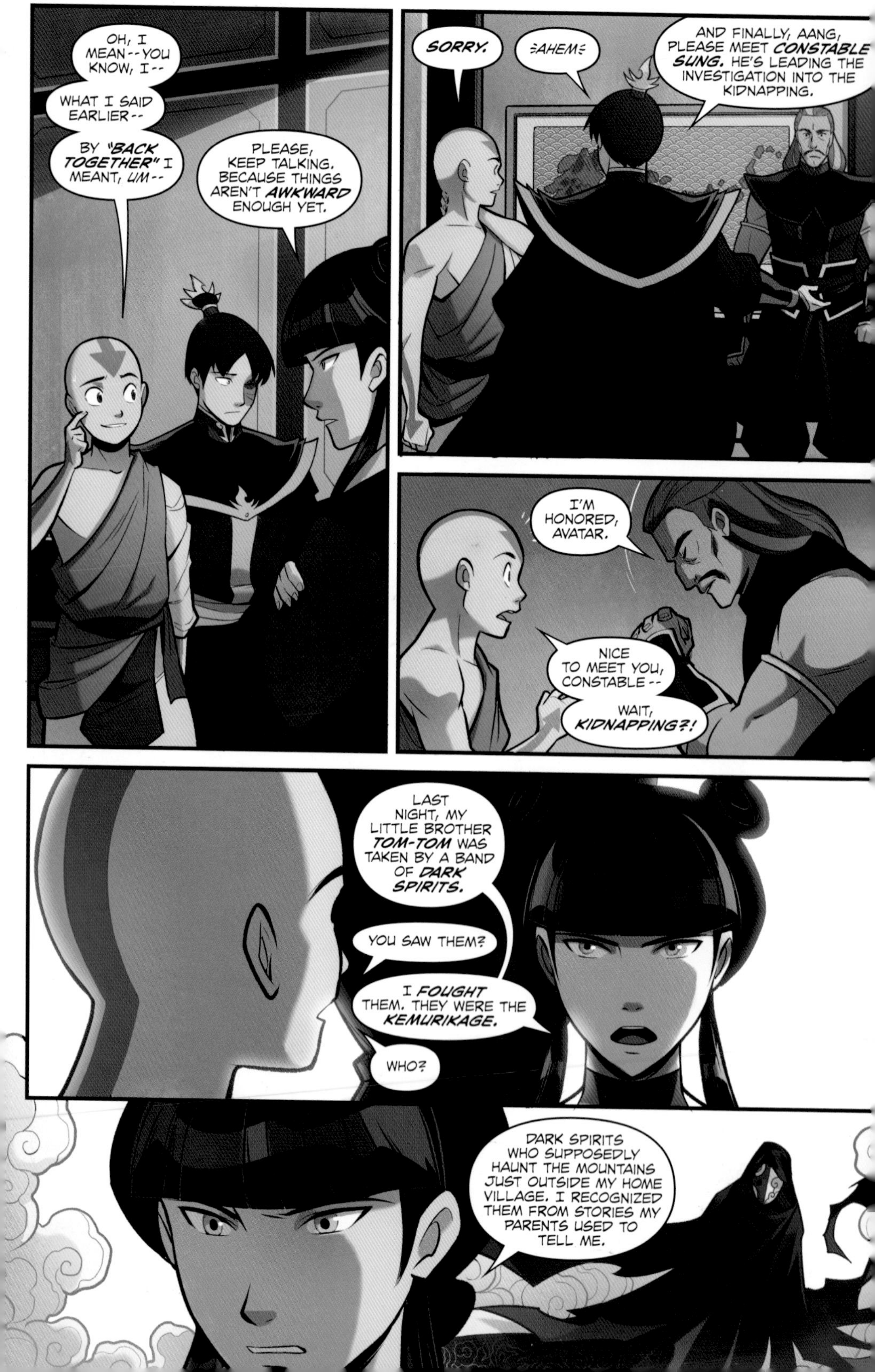
OH, I MEAN--YOU KNOW, I--
WHAT I SAID EARLIER--
BY "BACK TOGETHER" I MEANT, UM--
PLEASE, KEEP TALKING. BECAUSE THINGS AREN'T AWKWARD ENOUGH YET.
SORRY.
=AHEM=
AND FINALLY, AANG, PLEASE MEET CONSTABLE SUNG. HE'S LEADING THE INVESTIGATION INTO THE KIDNAPPING.
I'M HONORED, AVATAR.
NICE TO MEET YOU, CONSTABLE--
WAIT, KIDNAPPING?!
LAST NIGHT, MY LITTLE BROTHER TOM-TOM WAS TAKEN BY A BAND OF DARK SPIRITS.
YOU SAW THEM?
I FOUGHT THEM. THEY WERE THE KEMURIKAGE.
WHO?
DARK SPIRITS WHO SUPPOSEDLY HAUNT THE MOUNTAINS JUST OUTSIDE MY HOME VILLAGE. I RECOGNIZED THEM FROM STORIES MY PARENTS USED TO TELL ME.

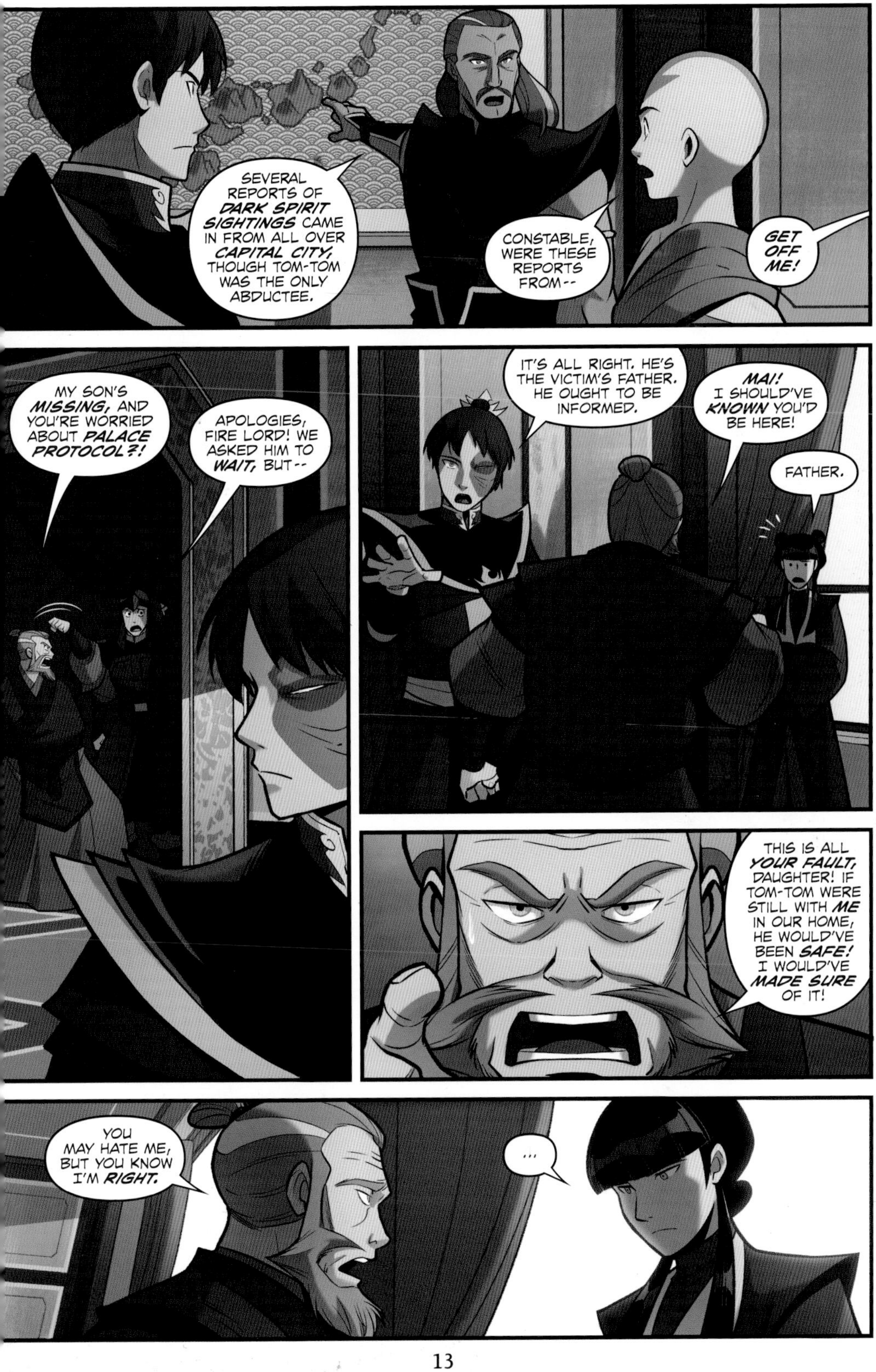
SEVERAL REPORTS OF DARK SPIRIT SIGHTINGS CAME IN FROM ALL OVER CAPITAL CITY, THOUGH TOM-TOM WAS THE ONLY ABDUCTEE.
CONSTABLE, WERE THESE REPORTS FROM--
GET OFF ME!
MY SON'S MISSING, AND YOU'RE WORRIED ABOUT PALACE PROTOCOL?!
APOLOGIES, FIRE LORD! WE ASKED HIM TO WAIT, BUT--
IT'S ALL RIGHT. HE'S THE VICTIM'S FATHER. HE OUGHT TO BE INFORMED.
MAI! I SHOULD'VE KNOWN YOU'D BE HERE!
FATHER.
THIS IS ALL YOUR FAULT, DAUGHTER! IF TOM-TOM WERE STILL WITH ME IN OUR HOME, HE WOULD'VE BEEN SAFE! I WOULD'VE MADE SURE OF IT!
YOU MAY HATE ME, BUT YOU KNOW I'M RIGHT.
...

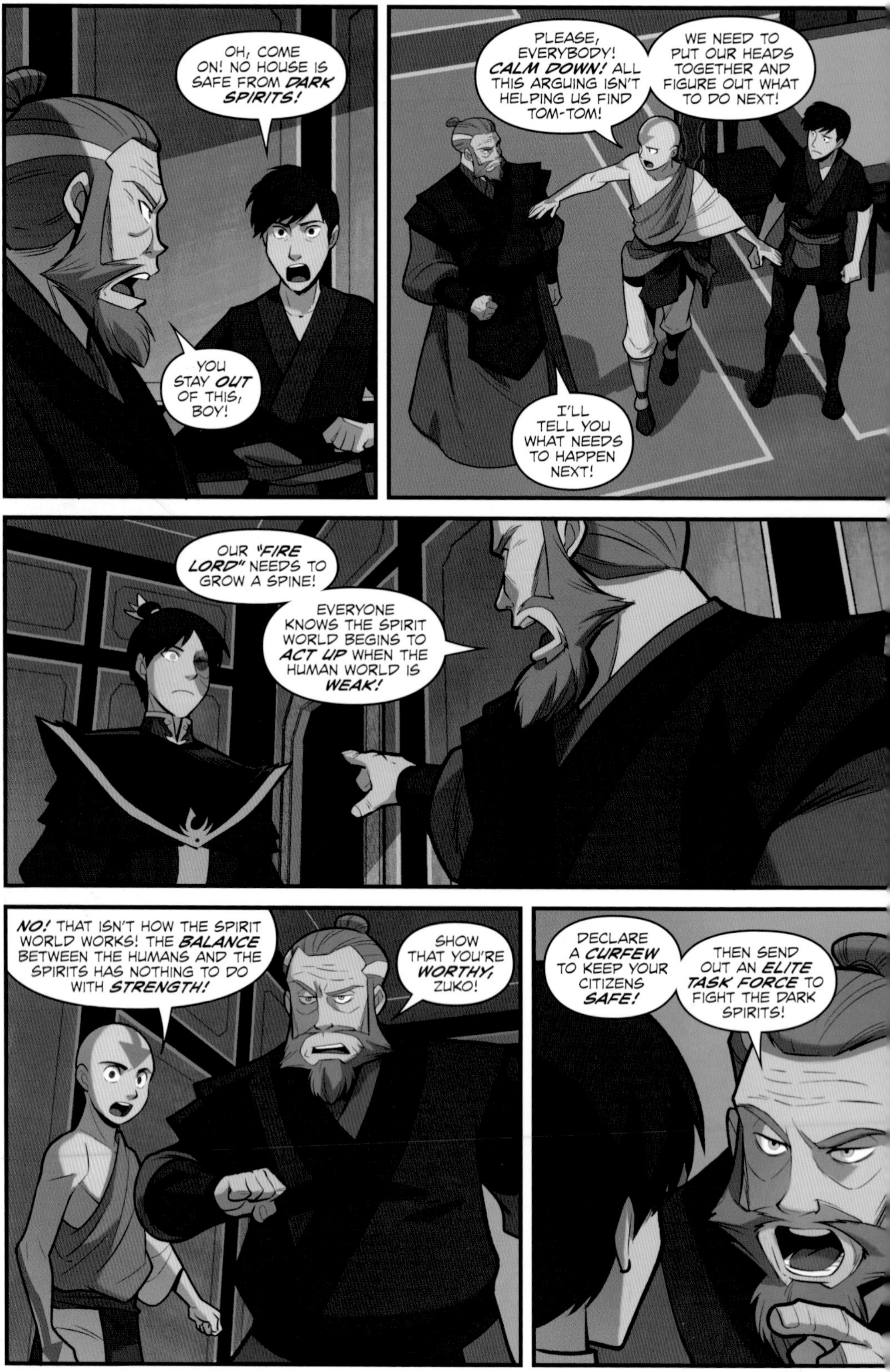
OH, COME ON! NO HOUSE IS SAFE FROM DARK SPIRITS!
YOU STAY OUT OF THIS, BOY!
PLEASE, EVERYBODY! CALM DOWN! ALL THIS ARGUING ISN'T HELPING US FIND TOM-TOM!
WE NEED TO PUT OUR HEADS TOGETHER AND FIGURE OUT WHAT TO DO NEXT!
I'LL TELL YOU WHAT NEEDS TO HAPPEN NEXT!
OUR "FIRE LORD" NEEDS TO GROW A SPINE!
EVERYONE KNOWS THE SPIRIT WORLD BEGINS TO ACT UP WHEN THE HUMAN WORLD IS WEAK!
NO! THAT ISN'T HOW THE SPIRIT WORLD WORKS! THE BALANCE BETWEEN THE HUMANS AND THE SPIRITS HAS NOTHING TO DO WITH STRENGTH!
SHOW THAT YOU'RE WORTHY, ZUKO!
DECLARE A CURFEW TO KEEP YOUR CITIZENS SAFE!
THEN SEND OUT AN ELITE TASK FORCE TO FIGHT THE DARK SPIRITS!

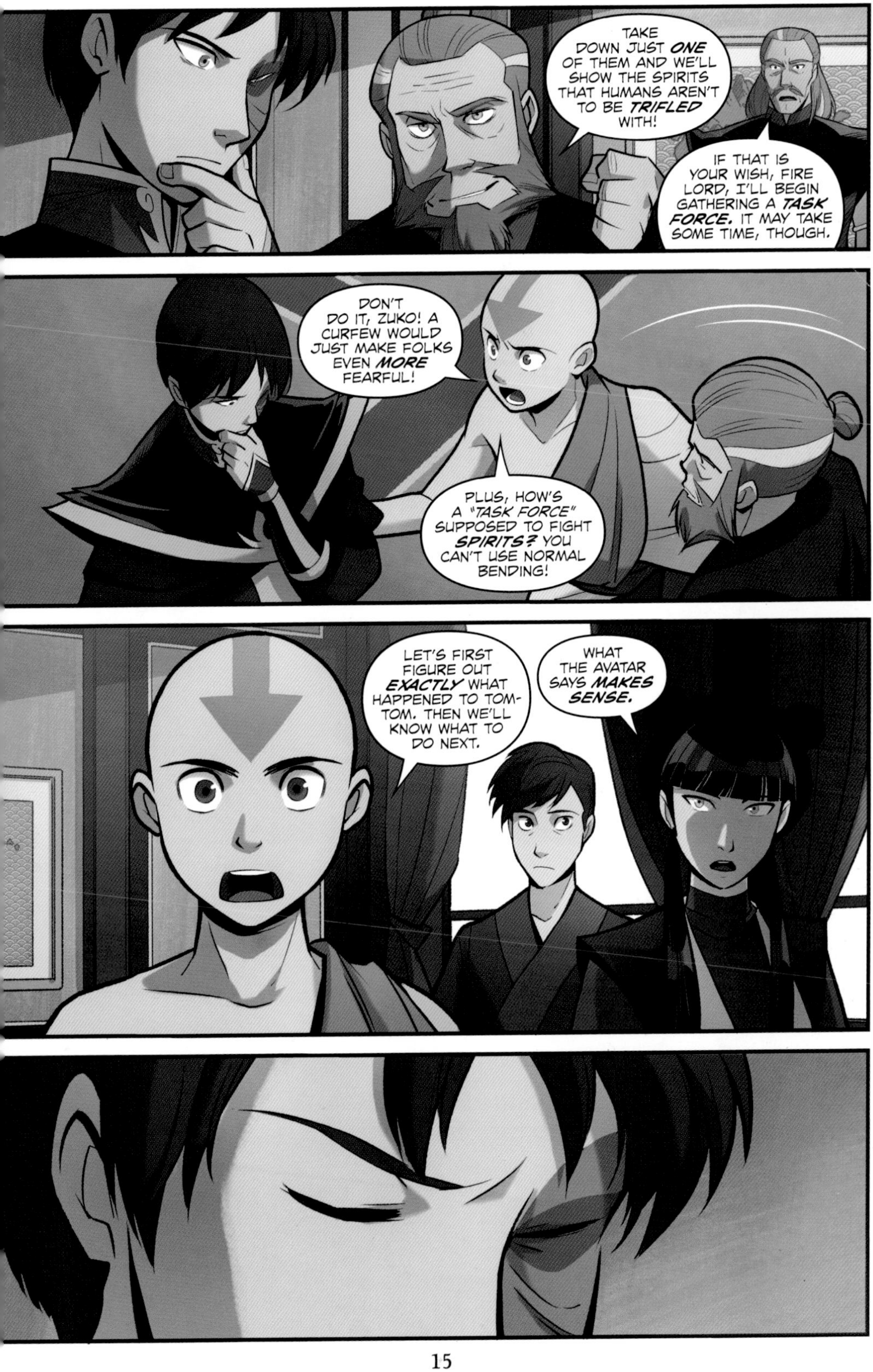
TAKE DOWN JUST ONE OF THEM AND WE'LL SHOW THE SPIRITS THAT HUMANS AREN'T TO BE TRIFLED WITH!
IF THAT IS YOUR WISH, FIRE LORD, I'LL BEGIN GATHERING A TASK FORCE. IT MAY TAKE SOME TIME, THOUGH.
DON'T DO IT, ZUKO! A CURFEW WOULD JUST MAKE FOLKS EVEN MORE FEARFUL!
PLUS, HOW'S A "TASK FORCE" SUPPOSED TO FIGHT SPIRITS? YOU CAN'T USE NORMAL BENDING!
LET'S FIRST FIGURE OUT EXACTLY WHAT HAPPENED TO TOM-TOM. THEN WE'LL KNOW WHAT TO DO NEXT.
WHAT THE AVATAR SAYS MAKES SENSE.

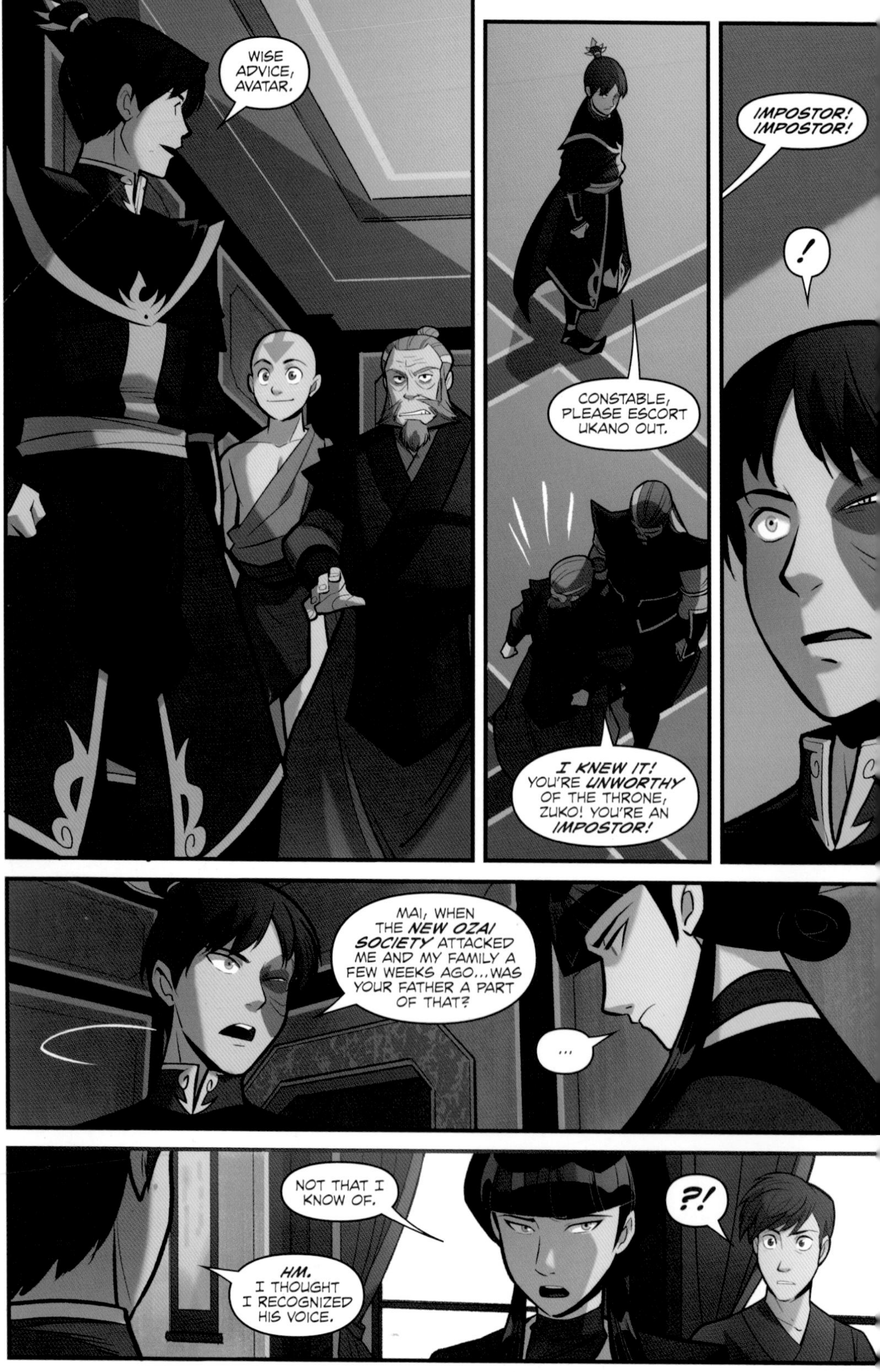
WISE ADVICE, AVATAR.
CONSTABLE, PLEASE ESCORT UKANO OUT.
I KNEW IT! YOU'RE UNWORTHY OF THE THRONE, ZUKO! YOU'RE AN IMPOSTOR!
IMPOSTOR! IMPOSTOR!
!
MAI, WHEN THE NEW OZAI SOCIETY ATTACKED ME AND MY FAMILY A FEW WEEKS AGO...WAS YOUR FATHER A PART OF THAT?
...
NOT THAT I KNOW OF.
HM. I THOUGHT I RECOGNIZED HIS VOICE.
?!

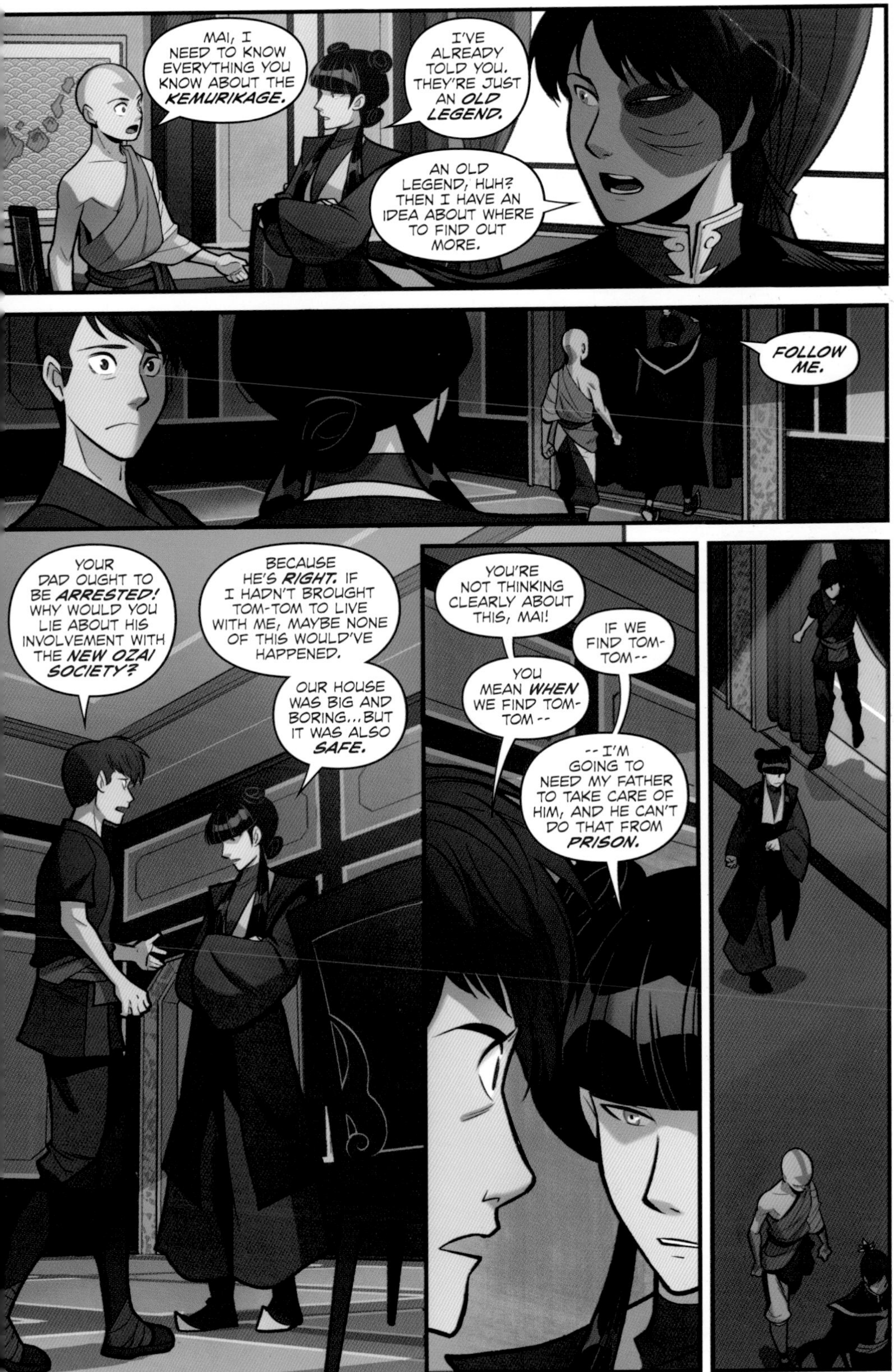
MAI, I NEED TO KNOW EVERYTHING YOU KNOW ABOUT THE KEMURIKAGE.
I'VE ALREADY TOLD YOU. THEY'RE JUST AN OLD LEGEND.
AN OLD LEGEND, HUH? THEN I HAVE AN IDEA ABOUT WHERE TO FIND OUT MORE.
FOLLOW ME.
YOUR DAD OUGHT TO BE ARRESTED! WHY WOULD YOU LIE ABOUT HIS INVOLVEMENT WITH THE NEW OZAI SOCIETY?
BECAUSE HE'S RIGHT. IF I HADN'T BROUGHT TOM-TOM TO LIVE WITH ME, MAYBE NONE OF THIS WOULD'VE HAPPENED.
OUR HOUSE WAS BIG AND BORING... BUT IT WAS ALSO SAFE.
YOU'RE NOT THINKING CLEARLY ABOUT THIS, MAI!
IF WE FIND TOM-TOM --
YOU MEAN WHEN WE FIND TOM-TOM --
-- I'M GOING TO NEED MY FATHER TO TAKE CARE OF HIM, AND HE CAN'T DO THAT FROM PRISON.

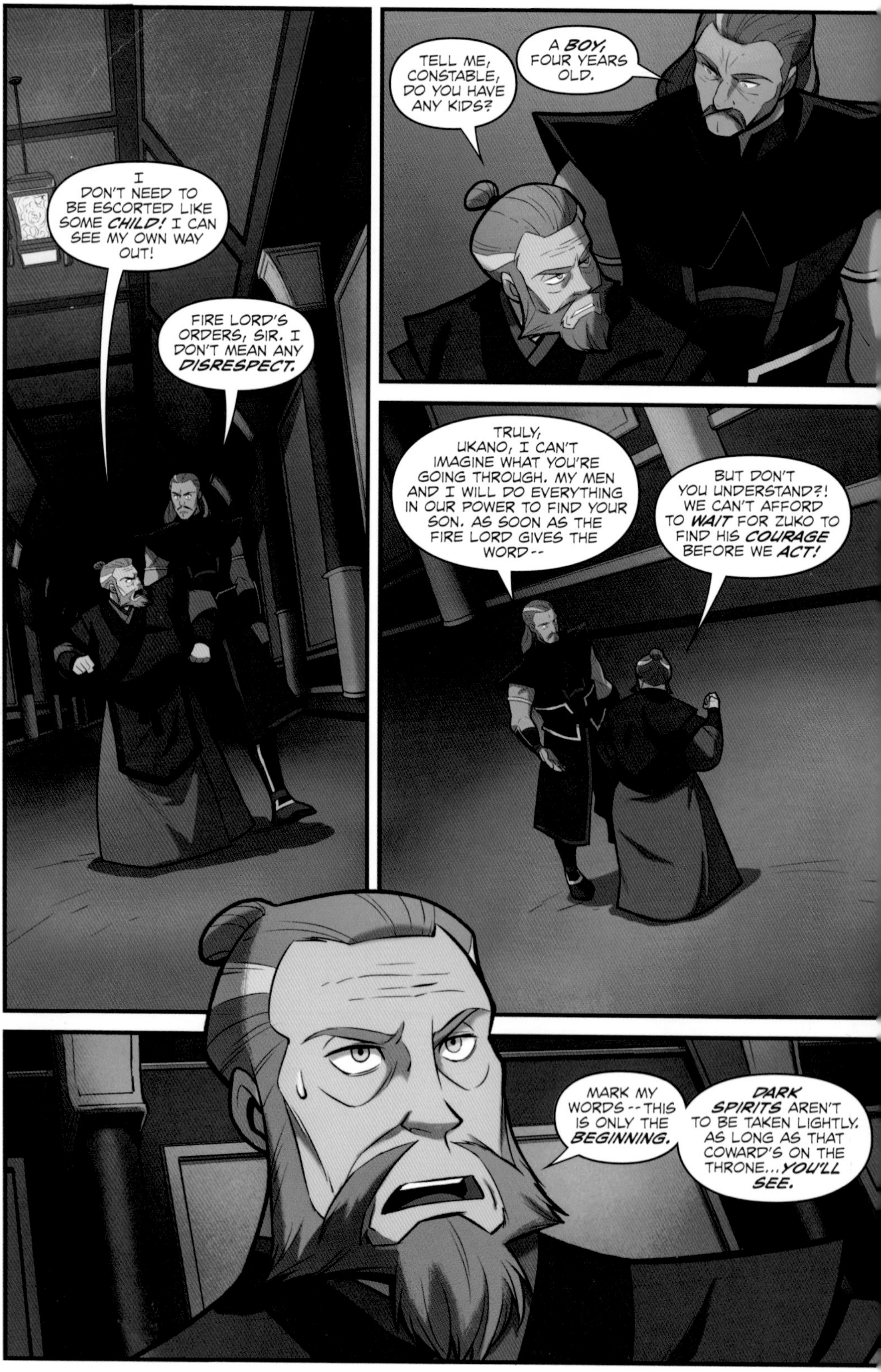
I DON'T NEED TO BE ESCORTED LIKE SOME CHILD! I CAN SEE MY OWN WAY OUT!
FIRE LORD'S ORDERS, SIR. I DON'T MEAN ANY DISRESPECT.
TELL ME, CONSTABLE, DO YOU HAVE ANY KIDS?
A BOY, FOUR YEARS OLD.
TRULY, UKANO, I CAN'T IMAGINE WHAT YOU'RE GOING THROUGH. MY MEN AND I WILL DO EVERYTHING IN OUR POWER TO FIND YOUR SON. AS SOON AS THE FIRE LORD GIVES THE WORD--
BUT DON'T YOU UNDERSTAND?! WE CAN'T AFFORD TO WAIT FOR ZUKO TO FIND HIS COURAGE BEFORE WE ACT!
MARK MY WORDS--THIS IS ONLY THE BEGINNING.
DARK SPIRITS AREN'T TO BE TAKEN LIGHTLY. AS LONG AS THAT COWARD'S ON THE THRONE...YOU'LL SEE.

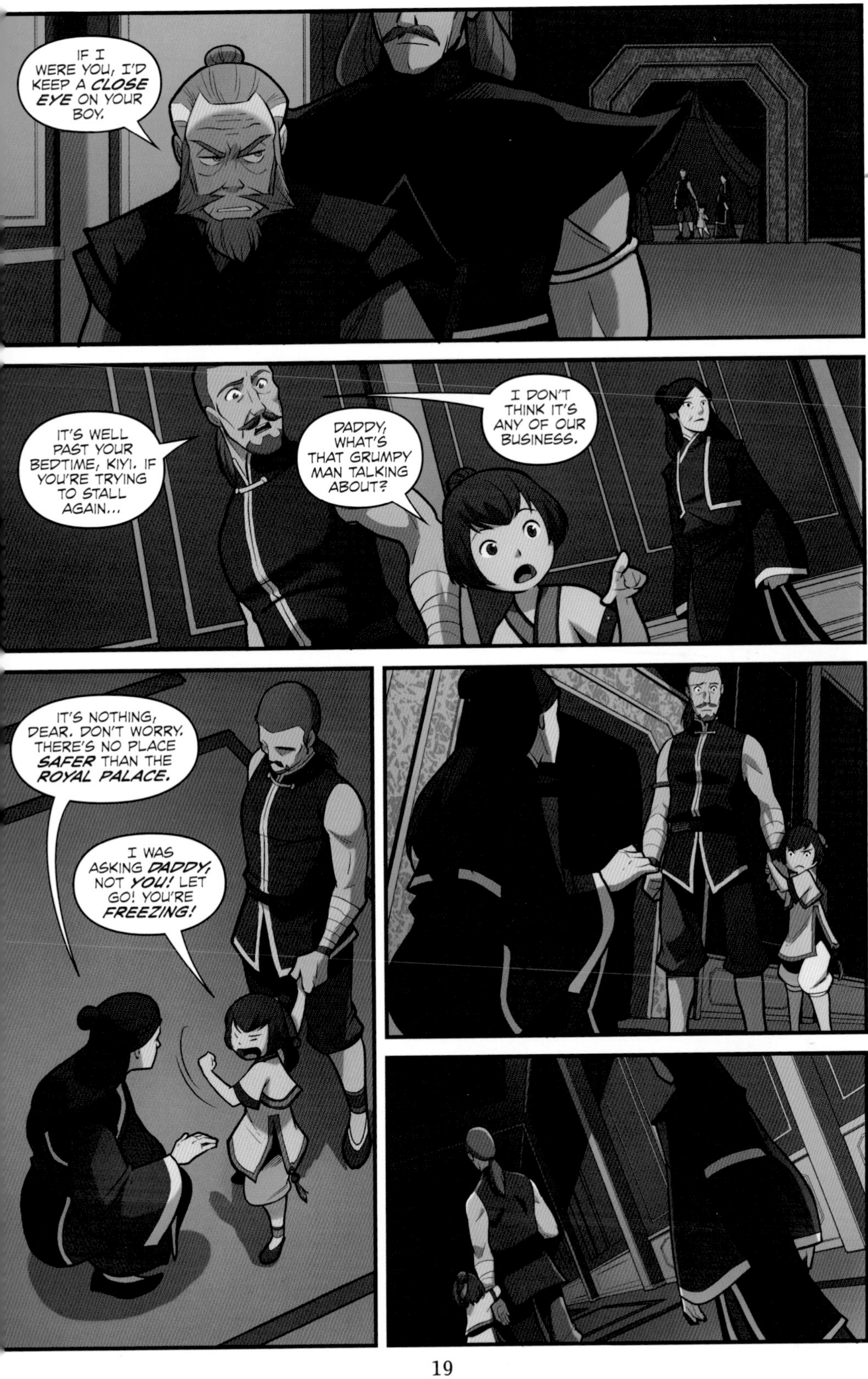
IF I WERE YOU, I'D KEEP A CLOSE EYE ON YOUR BOY.
IT'S WELL PAST YOUR BEDTIME, KIYI. IF YOU'RE TRYING TO STALL AGAIN...
DADDY, WHAT'S THAT GRUMPY MAN TALKING ABOUT?
I DON'T THINK IT'S ANY OF OUR BUSINESS.
IT'S NOTHING, DEAR. DON'T WORRY. THERE'S NO PLACE SAFER THAN THE ROYAL PALACE.
I WAS ASKING DADDY, NOT YOU! LET GO! YOU'RE FREEZING!

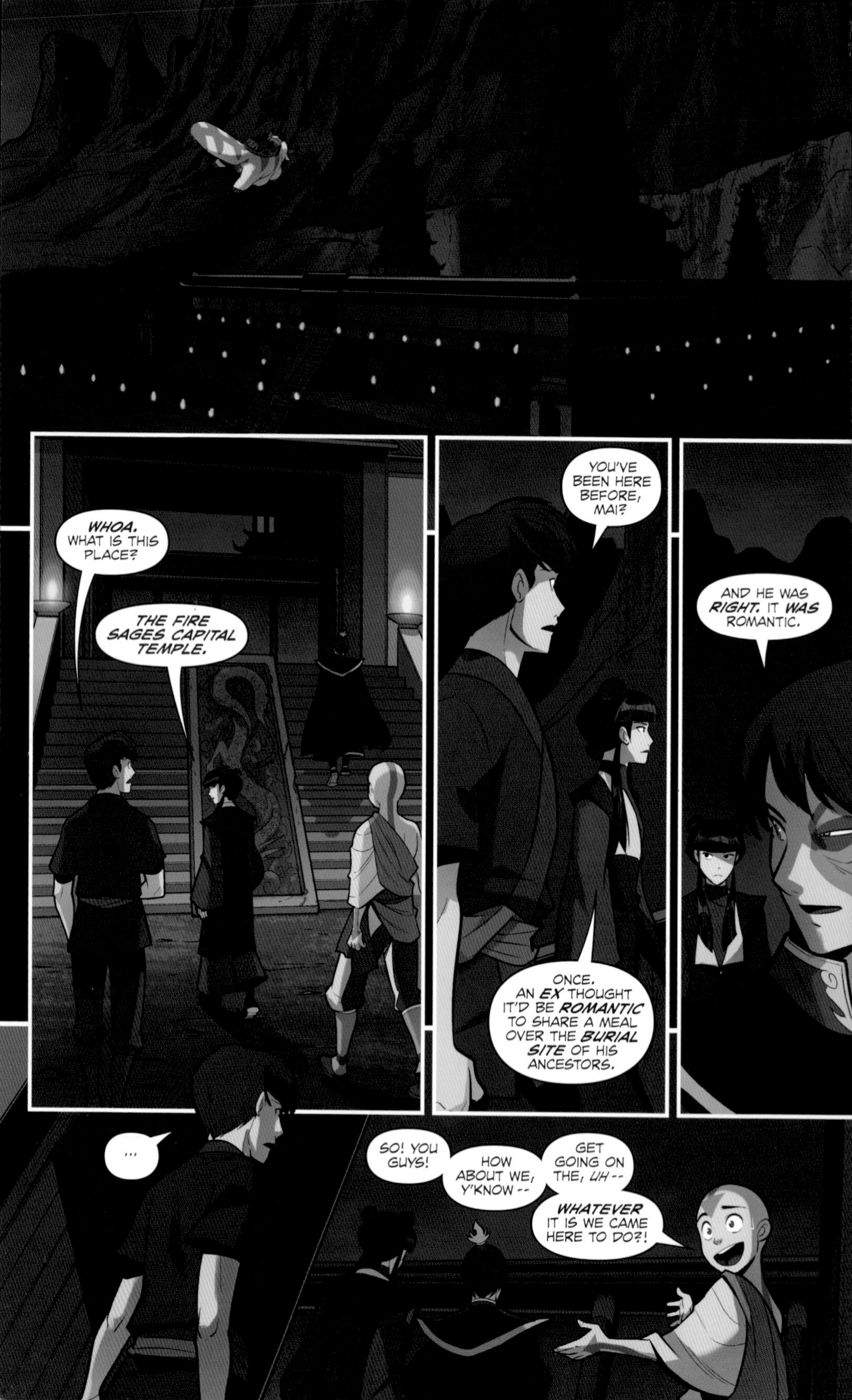

WHOA. WHAT IS THIS PLACE?
THE FIRE SAGES CAPITAL TEMPLE.
YOU'VE BEEN HERE BEFORE, MAI?
ONCE. AN EX THOUGHT IT'D BE ROMANTIC TO SHARE A MEAL OVER THE BURIAL SITE OF HIS ANCESTORS.
AND HE WAS RIGHT. IT WAS ROMANTIC.
...
SO! YOU GUYS!
HOW ABOUT WE, Y'KNOW --
GET GOING ON THE, UH --
WHATEVER IT IS WE CAME HERE TO DO?!

GREAT SAGE SHYU!

FIRE LORD! AVATAR! WHAT A PLEASANT SURPRISE!

SO GOOD TO SEE YOU AGAIN, SHYU!

I'M SORRY IT'S BEEN SO LONG SINCE MY LAST VISIT. THINGS HAVE BEEN *BUSY*.

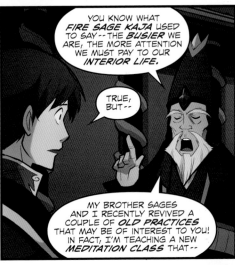

YOU KNOW WHAT *FIRE SAGE KAJA* USED TO SAY -- THE *BUSIER* WE ARE, THE MORE ATTENTION WE MUST PAY TO OUR *INTERIOR LIFE*.

TRUE, BUT--

MY BROTHER SAGES AND I RECENTLY REVIVED A COUPLE OF *OLD PRACTICES* THAT MAY BE OF INTEREST TO YOU! IN FACT, I'M TEACHING A NEW *MEDITATION CLASS* THAT--

I'D LOVE TO HEAR MORE, SHYU -- I SWEAR -- BUT RIGHT NOW, MY FRIENDS AND I NEED TO GET INTO THE *DRAGONBONE CATACOMBS*.

≡SIGH≡ OF COURSE.

DOES THE FIRE LORD VISIT OFTEN?

SURE. SOMETIMES FOR THE *VIEW*, SOMETIMES FOR THE *DUSTY OLD SCROLLS* IN THE CATACOMBS.

NEVER FOR MY *MEDITATION CLASSES*.

21

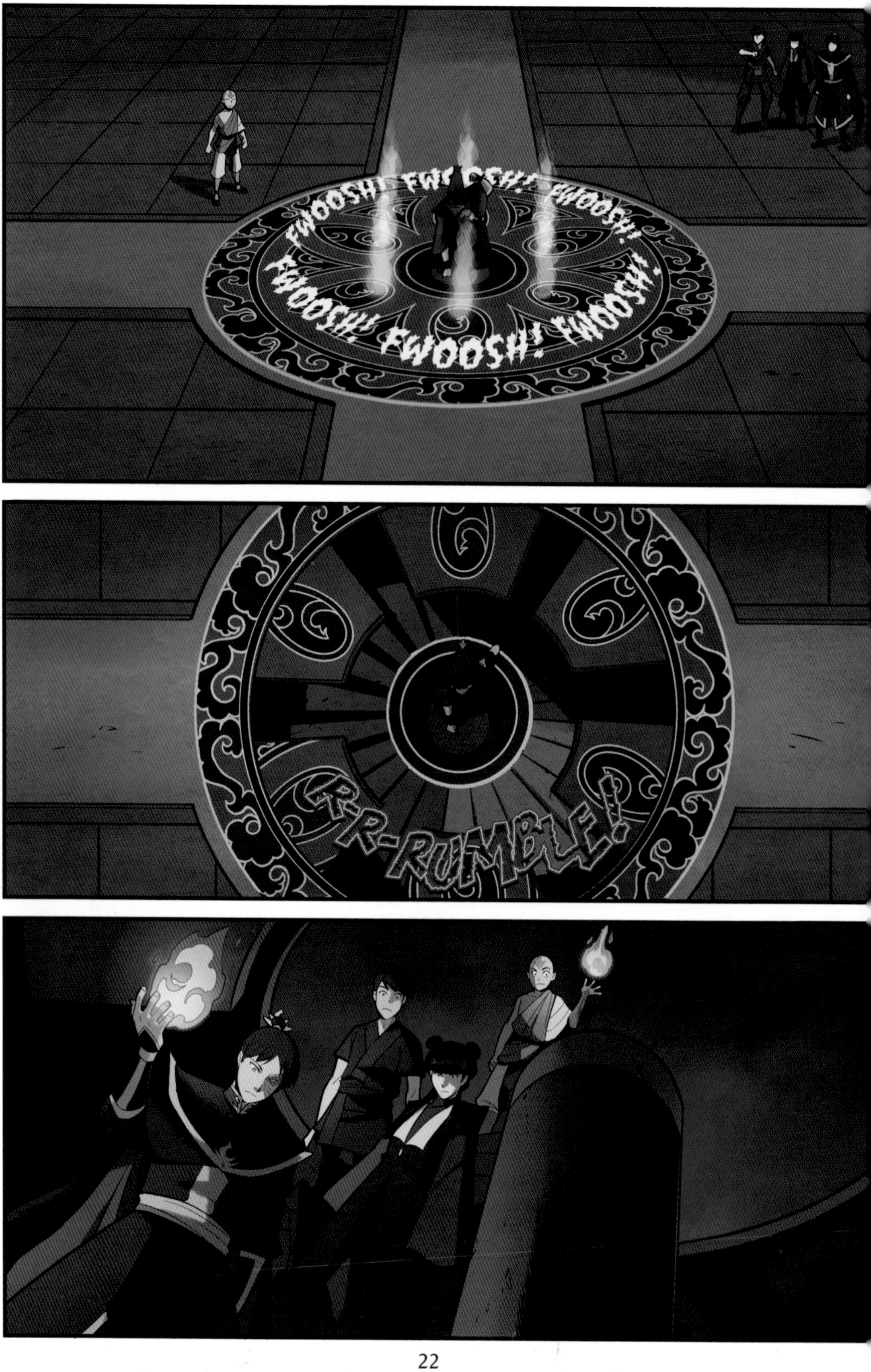
FWOOSH! FWOOSH! FWOOSH! FWOOSH! FWOOSH! FWOOSH!
R-R-RUMBLE!

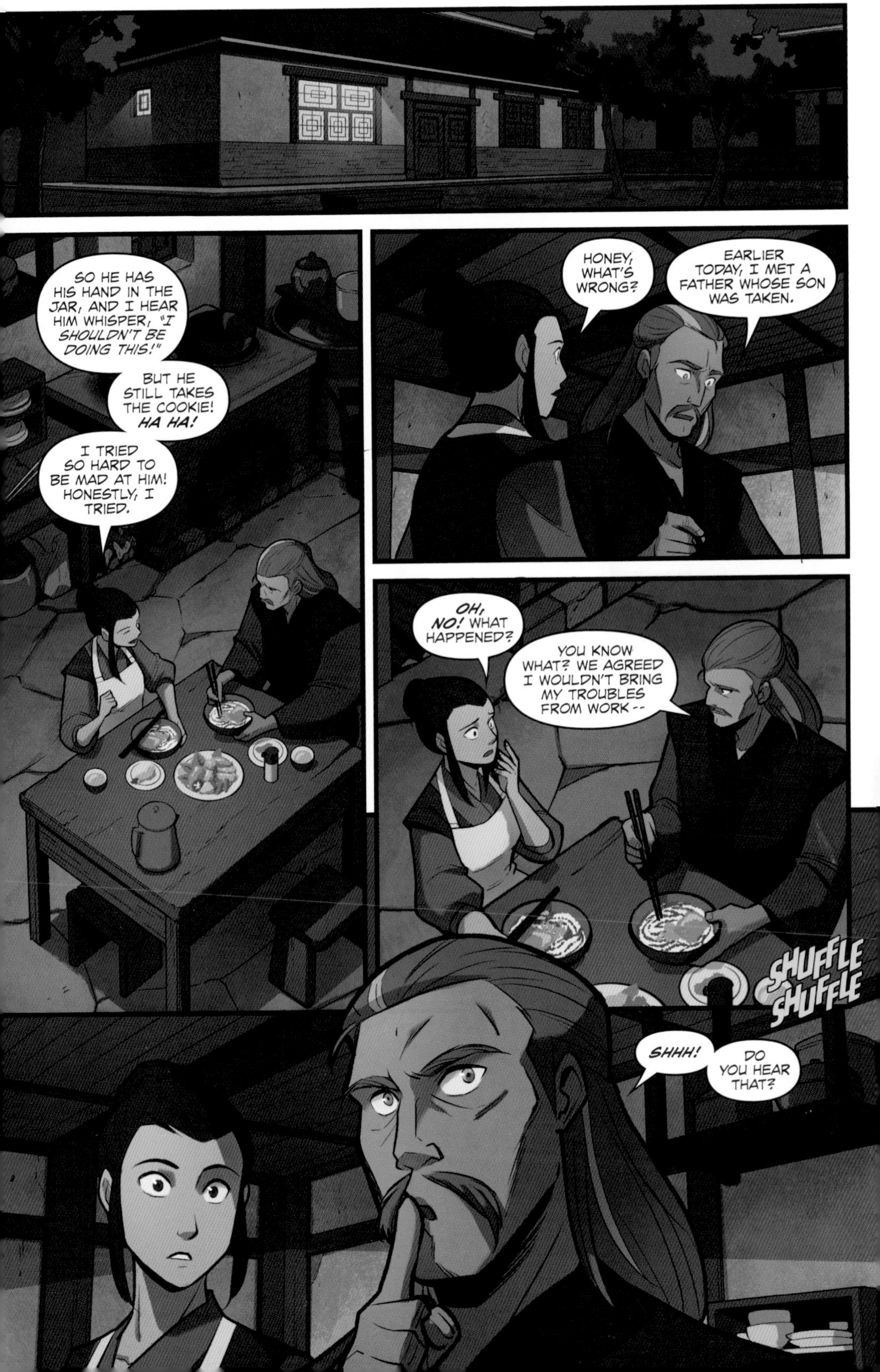
SO HE HAS HIS HAND IN THE JAR, AND I HEAR HIM WHISPER, "I SHOULDN'T BE DOING THIS!"
BUT HE STILL TAKES THE COOKIE! HA HA!
I TRIED SO HARD TO BE MAD AT HIM! HONESTLY, I TRIED.
HONEY, WHAT'S WRONG?
EARLIER TODAY, I MET A FATHER WHOSE SON WAS TAKEN.
OH, NO! WHAT HAPPENED?
YOU KNOW WHAT? WE AGREED I WOULDN'T BRING MY TROUBLES FROM WORK --
SHUFFLE SHUFFLE
SHHH!
DO YOU HEAR THAT?

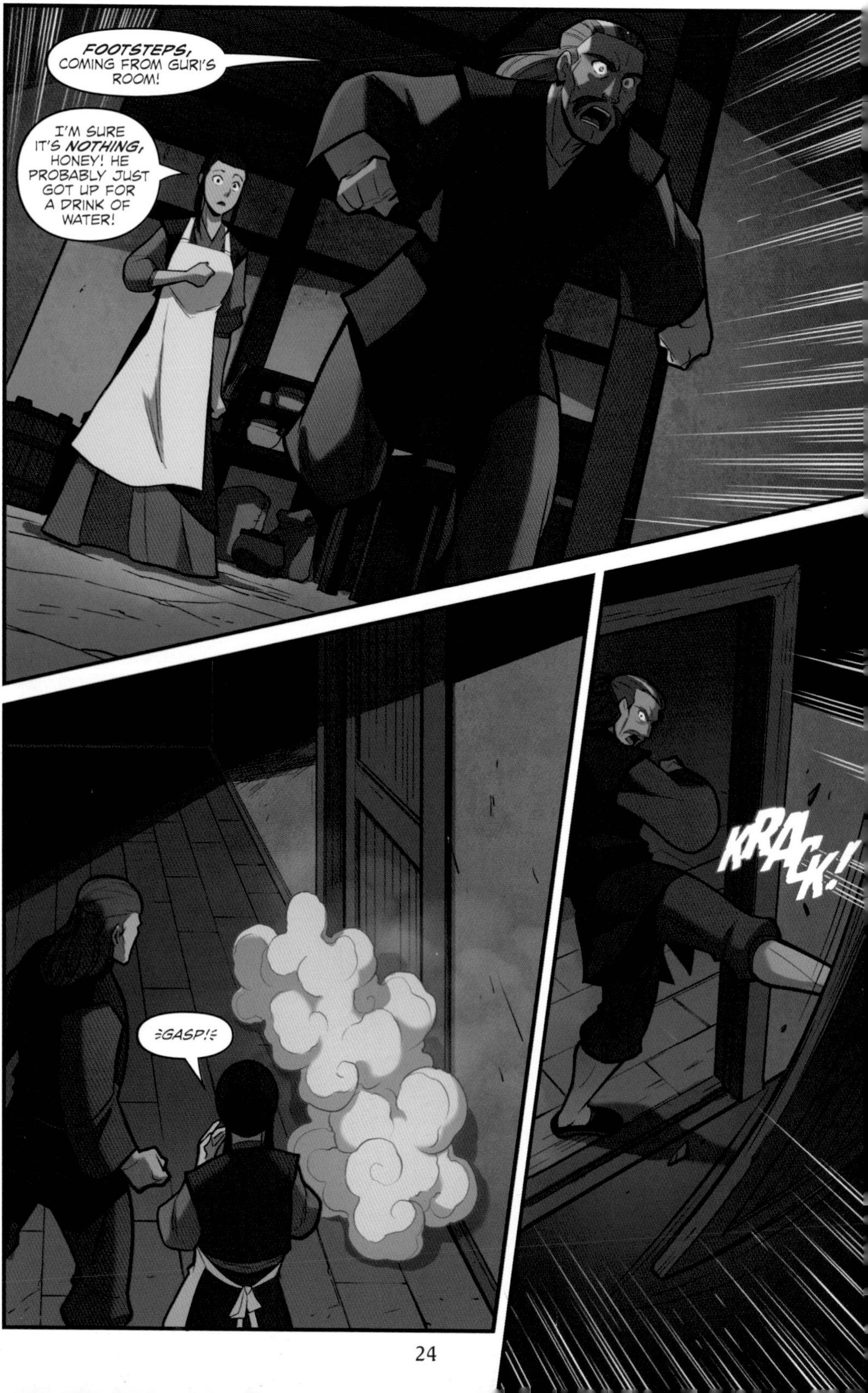
FOOTSTEPS, COMING FROM GURI'S ROOM!
I'M SURE IT'S NOTHING, HONEY! HE PROBABLY JUST GOT UP FOR A DRINK OF WATER!
GASP!
KRACK!

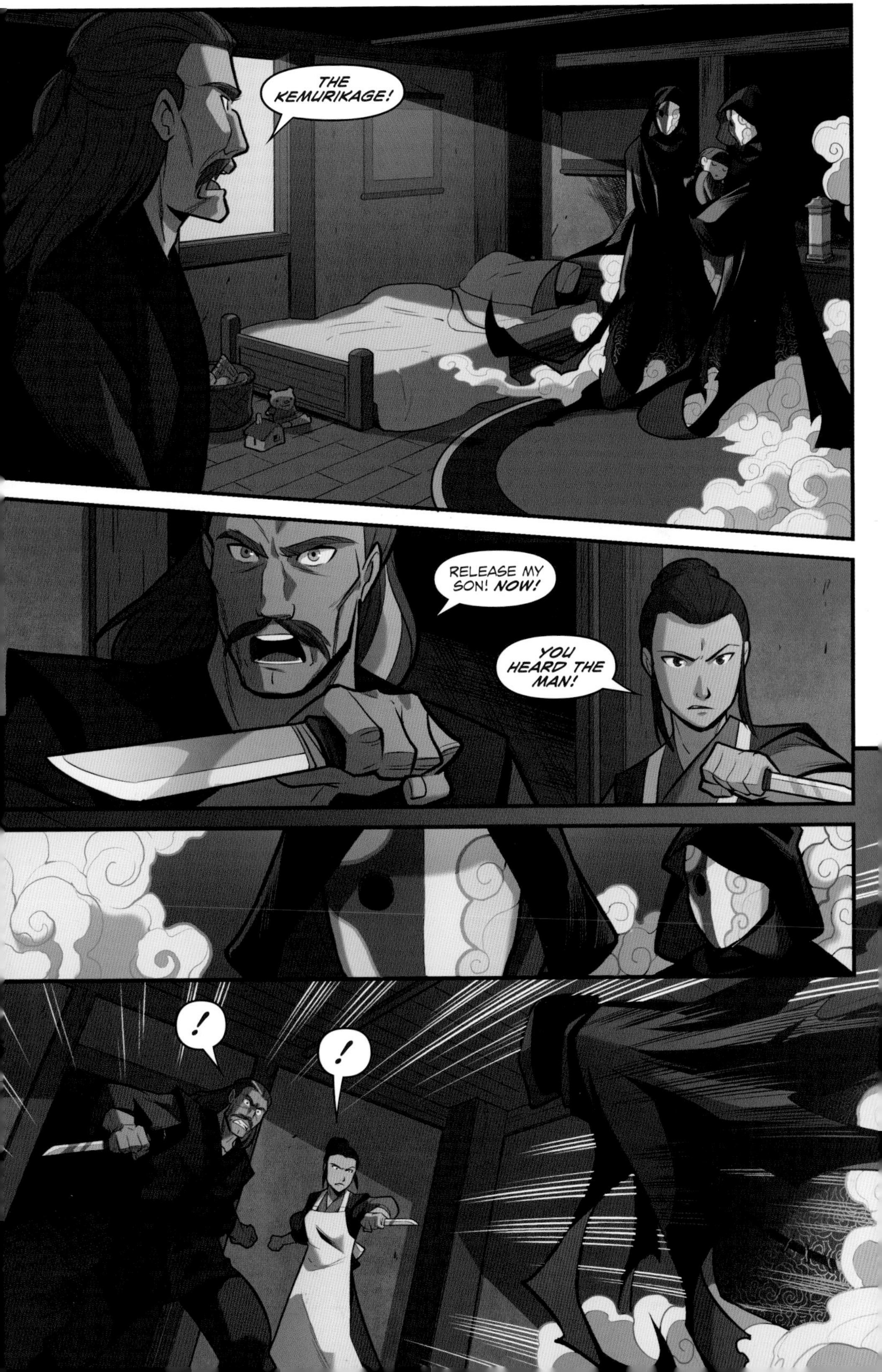
THE KEMURIKAGE!
RELEASE MY SON! NOW!
YOU HEARD THE MAN!
!
!

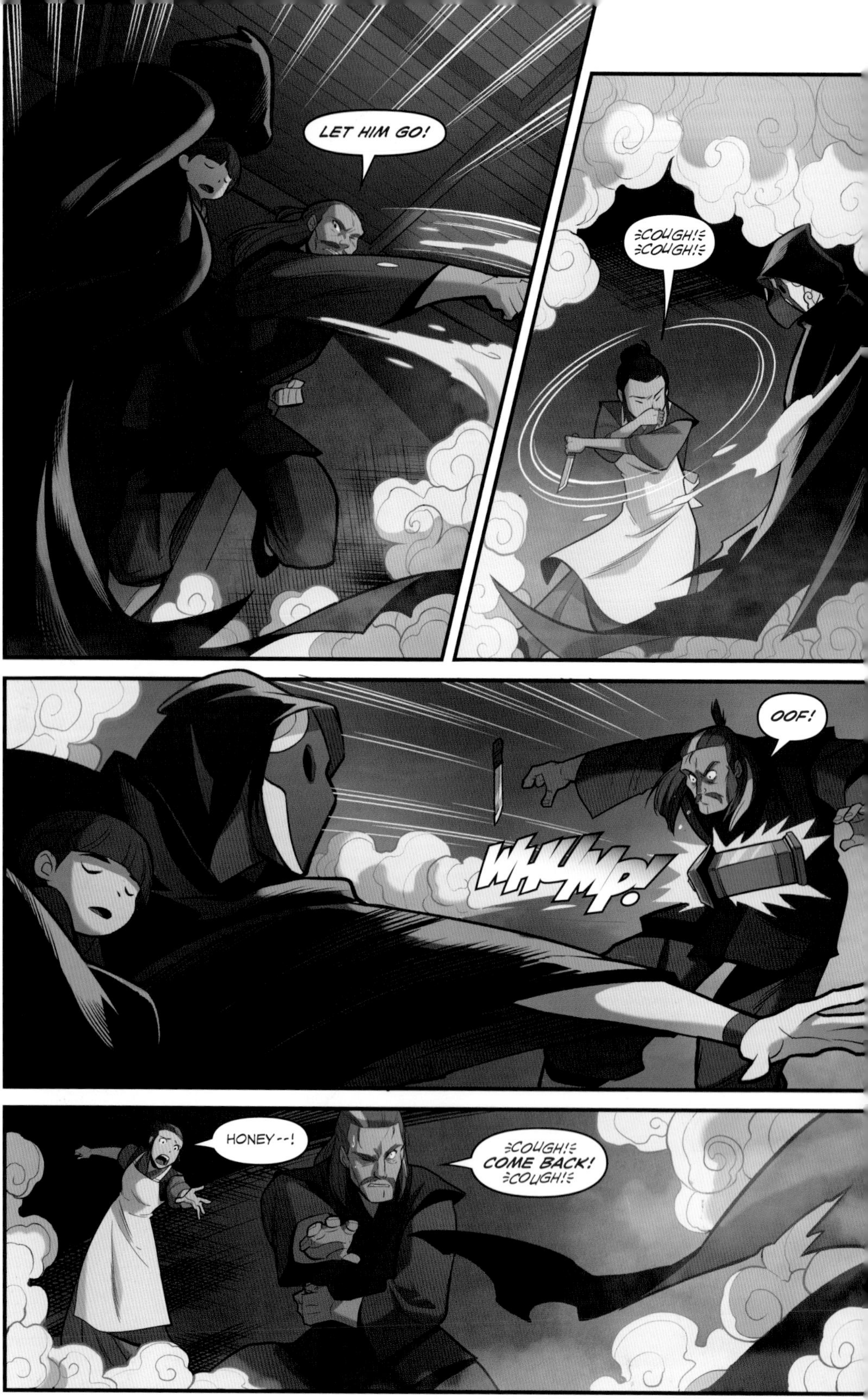
LET HIM GO!
COUGH! COUGH!
OOF!
WHUMP!
HONEY--!
COUGH! COME BACK! COUGH!

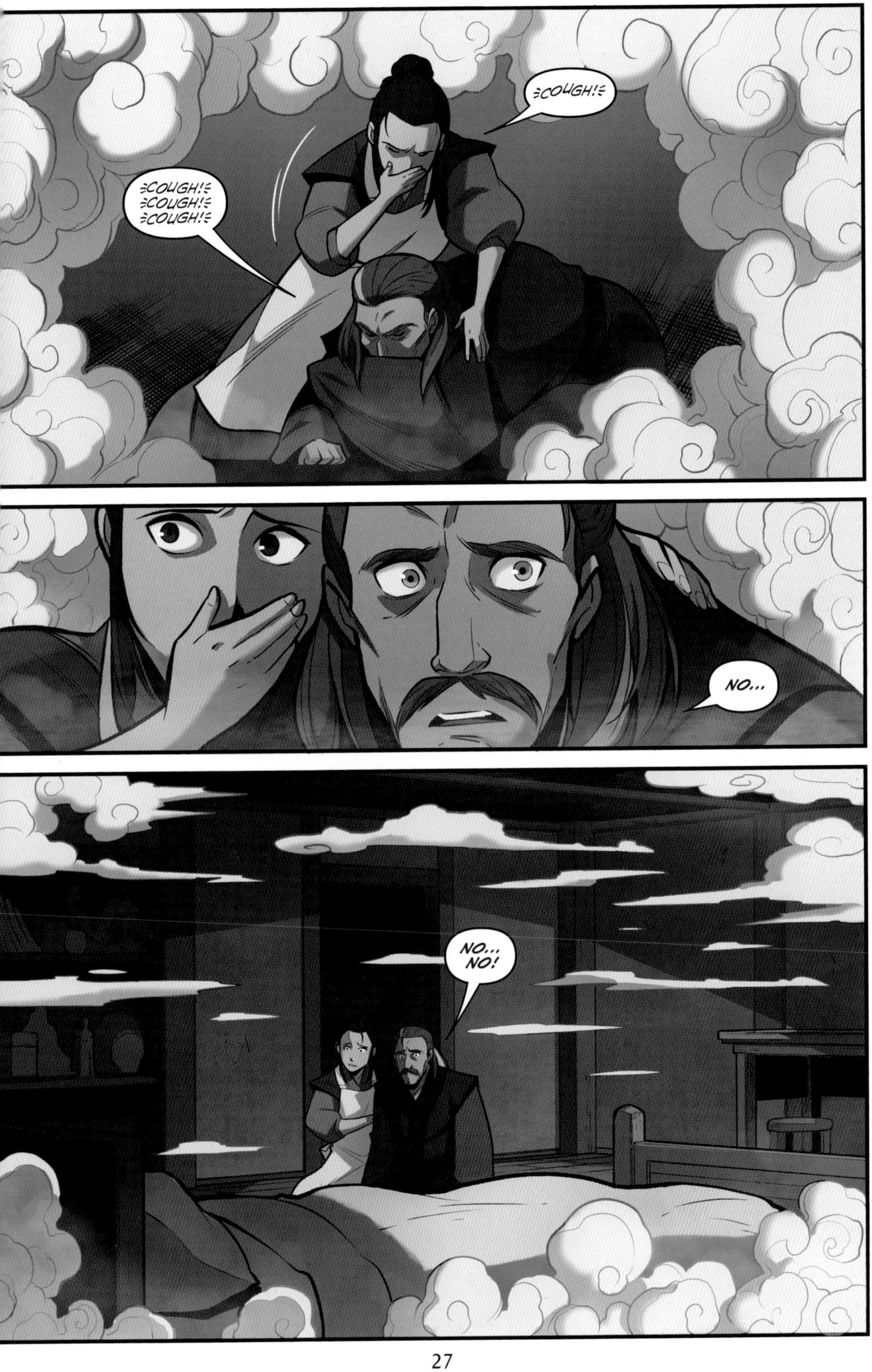

≈COUGH!≈
≈COUGH!≈
≈COUGH!≈
≈COUGH!≈
NO...
NO... NO!

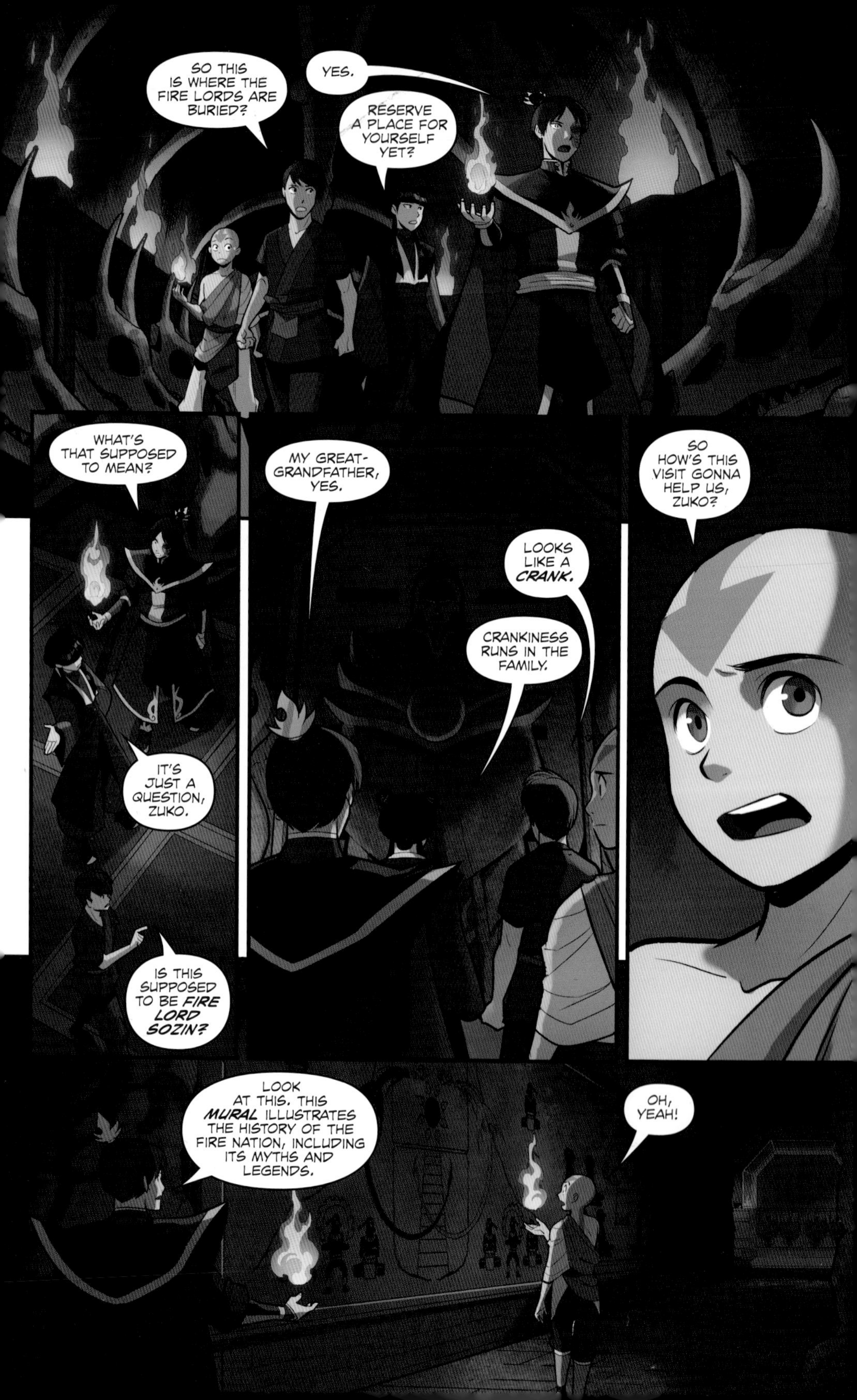

SO THIS IS WHERE THE FIRE LORDS ARE BURIED?
YES.
RESERVE A PLACE FOR YOURSELF YET?
WHAT'S THAT SUPPOSED TO MEAN?
IT'S JUST A QUESTION, ZUKO.
IS THIS SUPPOSED TO BE *FIRE LORD SOZIN?*
MY GREAT-GRANDFATHER, YES.
LOOKS LIKE A *CRANK.*
CRANKINESS RUNS IN THE FAMILY.
SO HOW'S THIS VISIT GONNA HELP US, ZUKO?
LOOK AT THIS. THIS *MURAL* ILLUSTRATES THE HISTORY OF THE FIRE NATION, INCLUDING ITS MYTHS AND LEGENDS.
OH, YEAH!

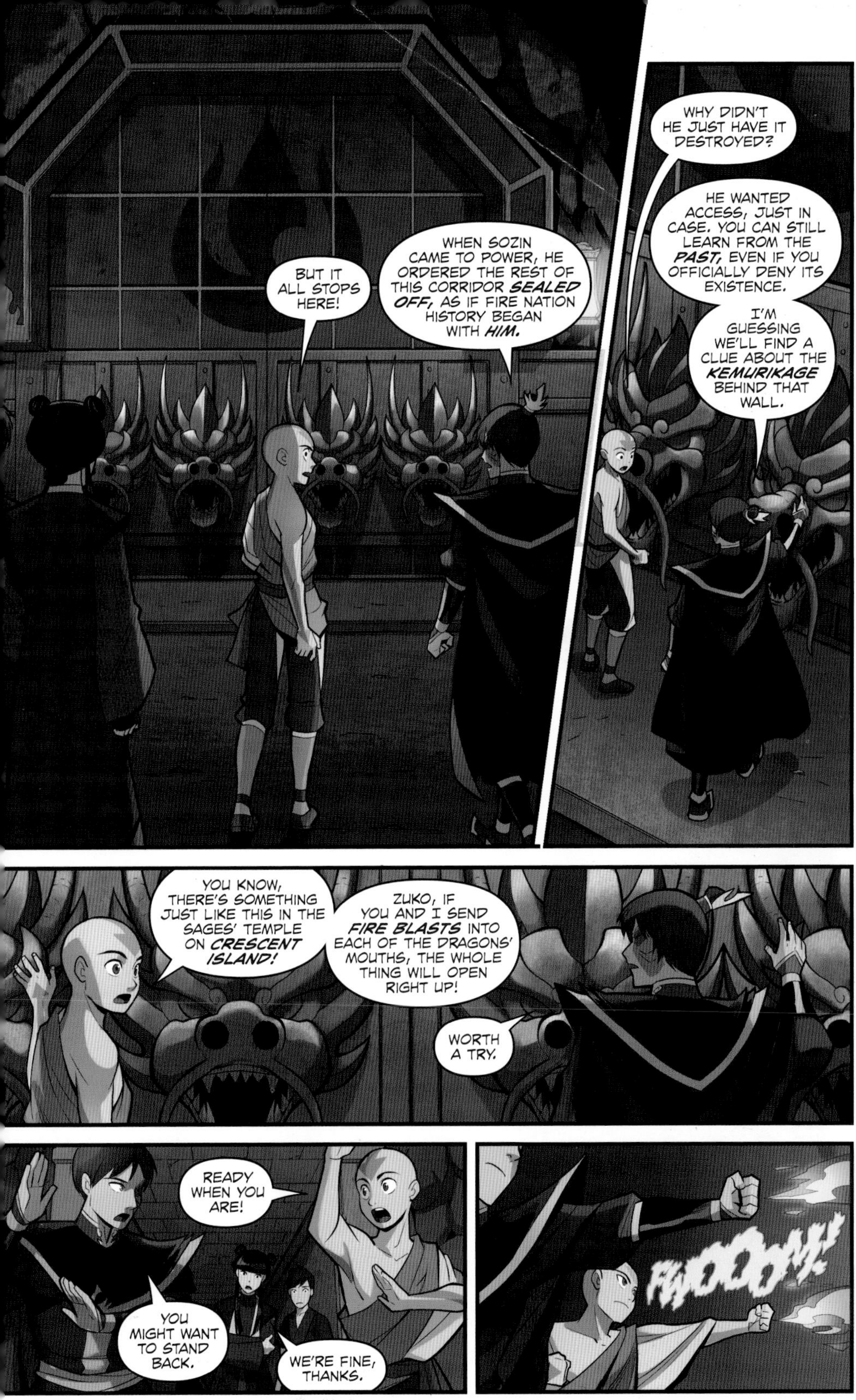
BUT IT ALL STOPS HERE!
WHEN SOZIN CAME TO POWER, HE ORDERED THE REST OF THIS CORRIDOR SEALED OFF, AS IF FIRE NATION HISTORY BEGAN WITH HIM.
WHY DIDN'T HE JUST HAVE IT DESTROYED?
HE WANTED ACCESS, JUST IN CASE. YOU CAN STILL LEARN FROM THE PAST, EVEN IF YOU OFFICIALLY DENY ITS EXISTENCE.
I'M GUESSING WE'LL FIND A CLUE ABOUT THE KEMURIKAGE BEHIND THAT WALL.
YOU KNOW, THERE'S SOMETHING JUST LIKE THIS IN THE SAGES' TEMPLE ON CRESCENT ISLAND!
ZUKO, IF YOU AND I SEND FIRE BLASTS INTO EACH OF THE DRAGONS' MOUTHS, THE WHOLE THING WILL OPEN RIGHT UP!
WORTH A TRY.
READY WHEN YOU ARE!
YOU MIGHT WANT TO STAND BACK.
WE'RE FINE, THANKS.
FWOOOM!

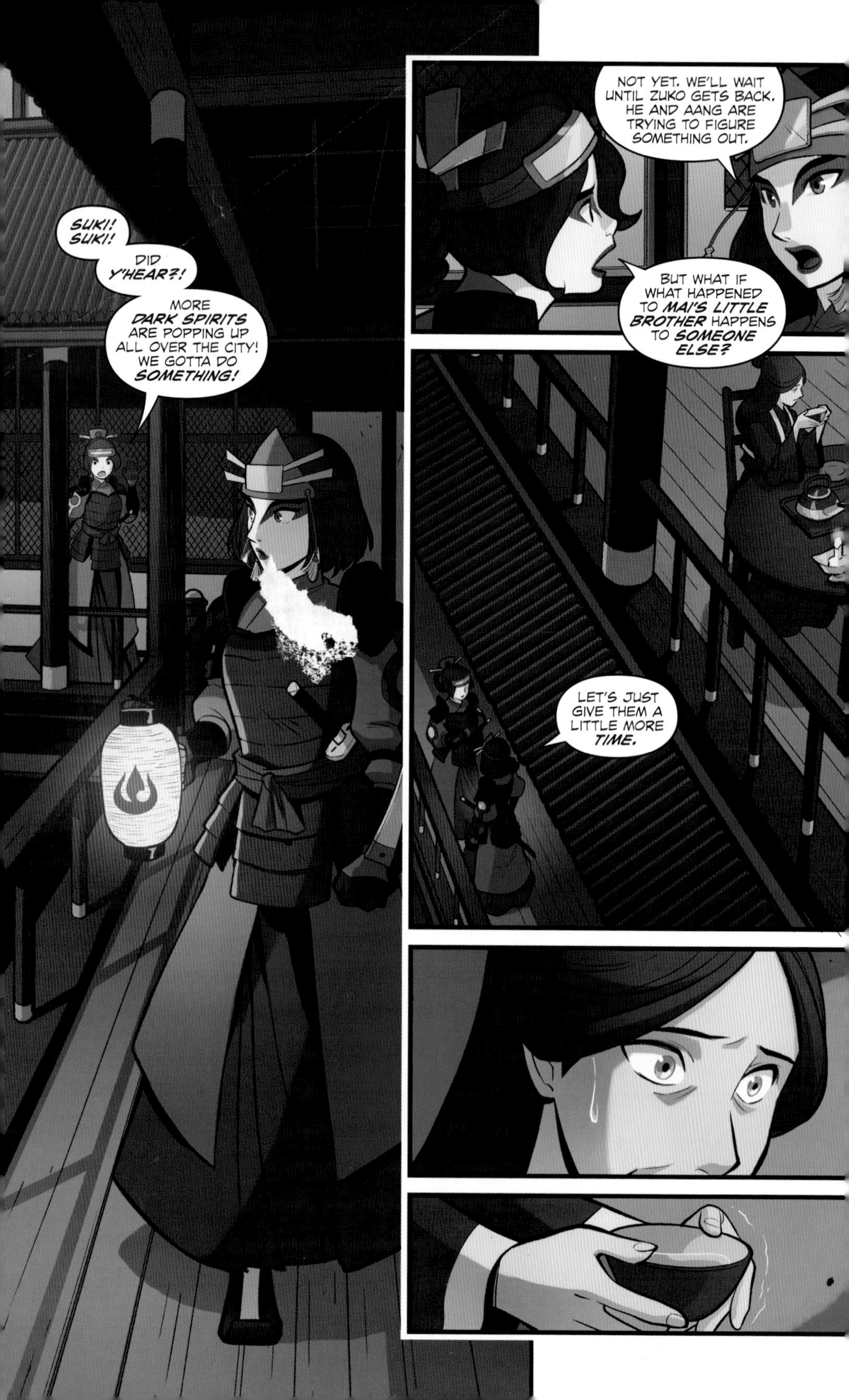
SUKI! SUKI!
DID Y'HEAR?!
MORE DARK SPIRITS ARE POPPING UP ALL OVER THE CITY! WE GOTTA DO SOMETHING!
NOT YET. WE'LL WAIT UNTIL ZUKO GETS BACK. HE AND AANG ARE TRYING TO FIGURE SOMETHING OUT.
BUT WHAT IF WHAT HAPPENED TO MAI'S LITTLE BROTHER HAPPENS TO SOMEONE ELSE?
LET'S JUST GIVE THEM A LITTLE MORE TIME.

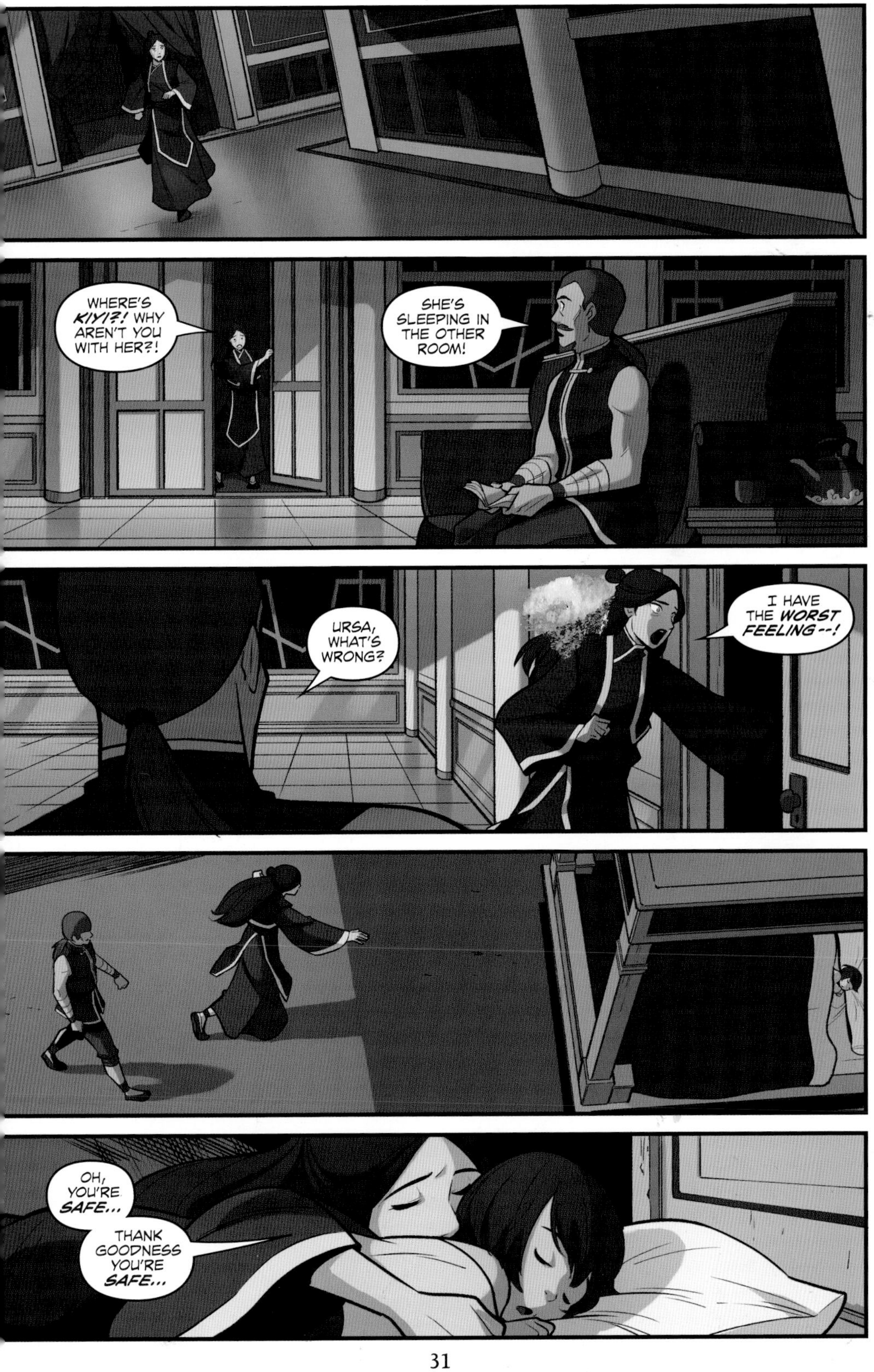
WHERE'S KIYI?! WHY AREN'T YOU WITH HER?!
SHE'S SLEEPING IN THE OTHER ROOM!
URSA, WHAT'S WRONG?
I HAVE THE WORST FEELING--!
OH, YOU'RE SAFE...
THANK GOODNESS YOU'RE SAFE...

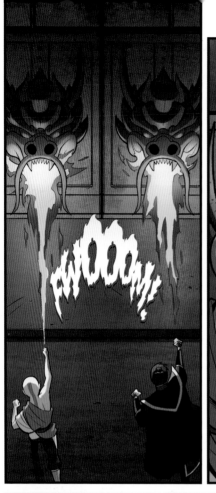

NOTHING.

HUH. MAYBE IF WE GIVE IT ONE MORE TRY--

YOU'VE GIVEN IT, LIKE, *TWENTY TRIES* ALREADY! *MY TURN.*

I DIDN'T KNOW YOU COULD FIREBEND, KEI LO.

I CAN'T. MAI, CAN I BORROW FOUR OF YOUR THROWING KNIVES?

IF YOU TWO HAD TAKEN THE TIME TO STUDY THE DRAGONS -- INSTEAD OF JUST BLASTING AWAY -- YOU WOULD'VE NOTICED THAT THE LOCKING MECHANISMS AREN'T LOCATED IN THE DRAGONS' MOUTHS.

WAIT, YOU'RE GONNA PICK THE DRAGONS' *NOSES?* THAT SEEMS AWFULLY *DISRESPECTFUL.*

NOT TO MENTION *GROSS.*

BABE, CAN YOU HELP ME OUT HERE?

SURE.

"BABE"?

YOU'RE NOT REALLY ONE TO TALK, AANG.

JUST HOLD THIS *HERE* --

-- AND THIS *HERE*.

GIVE EACH A COUNTER-CLOCKWISE TWIST --

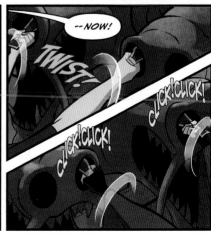

-- NOW!

TWIST!

CLICK! CLICK!

CLICK! CLICK!

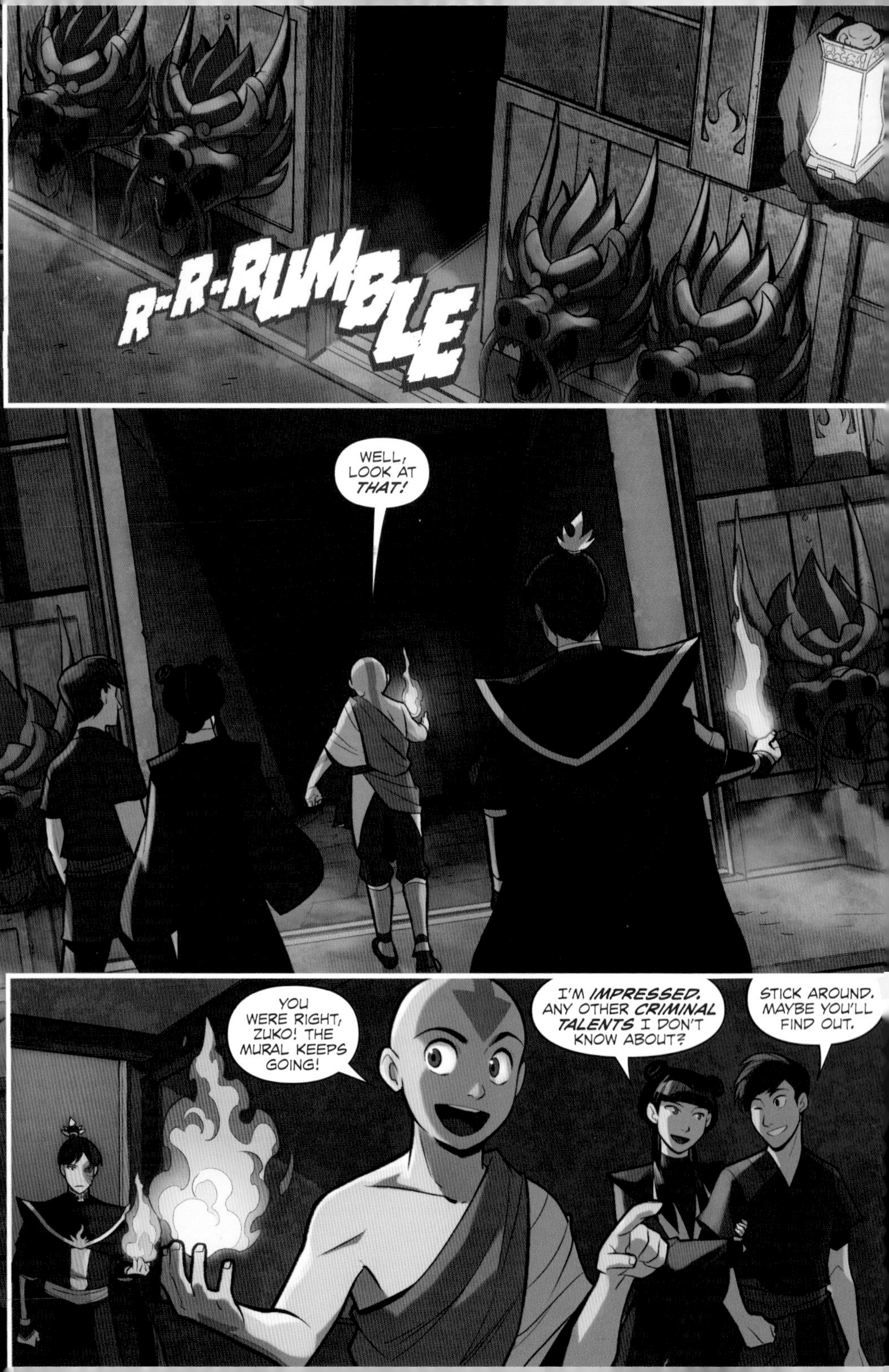
R-R-RUMBLE
WELL, LOOK AT *THAT!*
YOU WERE RIGHT, ZUKO! THE MURAL KEEPS GOING!
I'M *IMPRESSED.* ANY OTHER *CRIMINAL TALENTS* I DON'T KNOW ABOUT?
STICK AROUND. MAYBE YOU'LL FIND OUT.

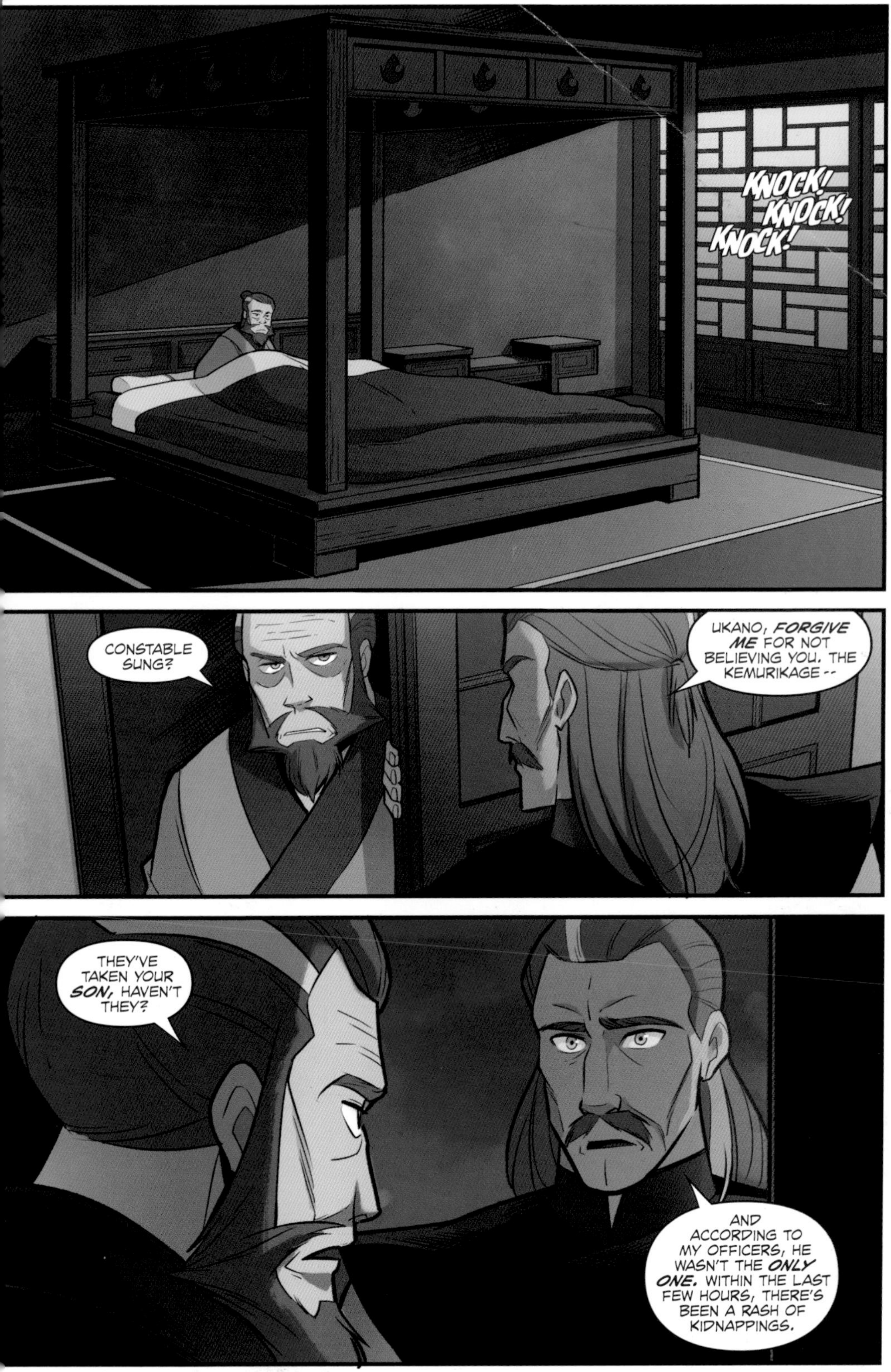
KNOCK! KNOCK! KNOCK!
CONSTABLE SUNG?
UKANO, FORGIVE ME FOR NOT BELIEVING YOU. THE KEMURIKAGE--
THEY'VE TAKEN YOUR SON, HAVEN'T THEY?
AND ACCORDING TO MY OFFICERS, HE WASN'T THE ONLY ONE. WITHIN THE LAST FEW HOURS, THERE'S BEEN A RASH OF KIDNAPPINGS.

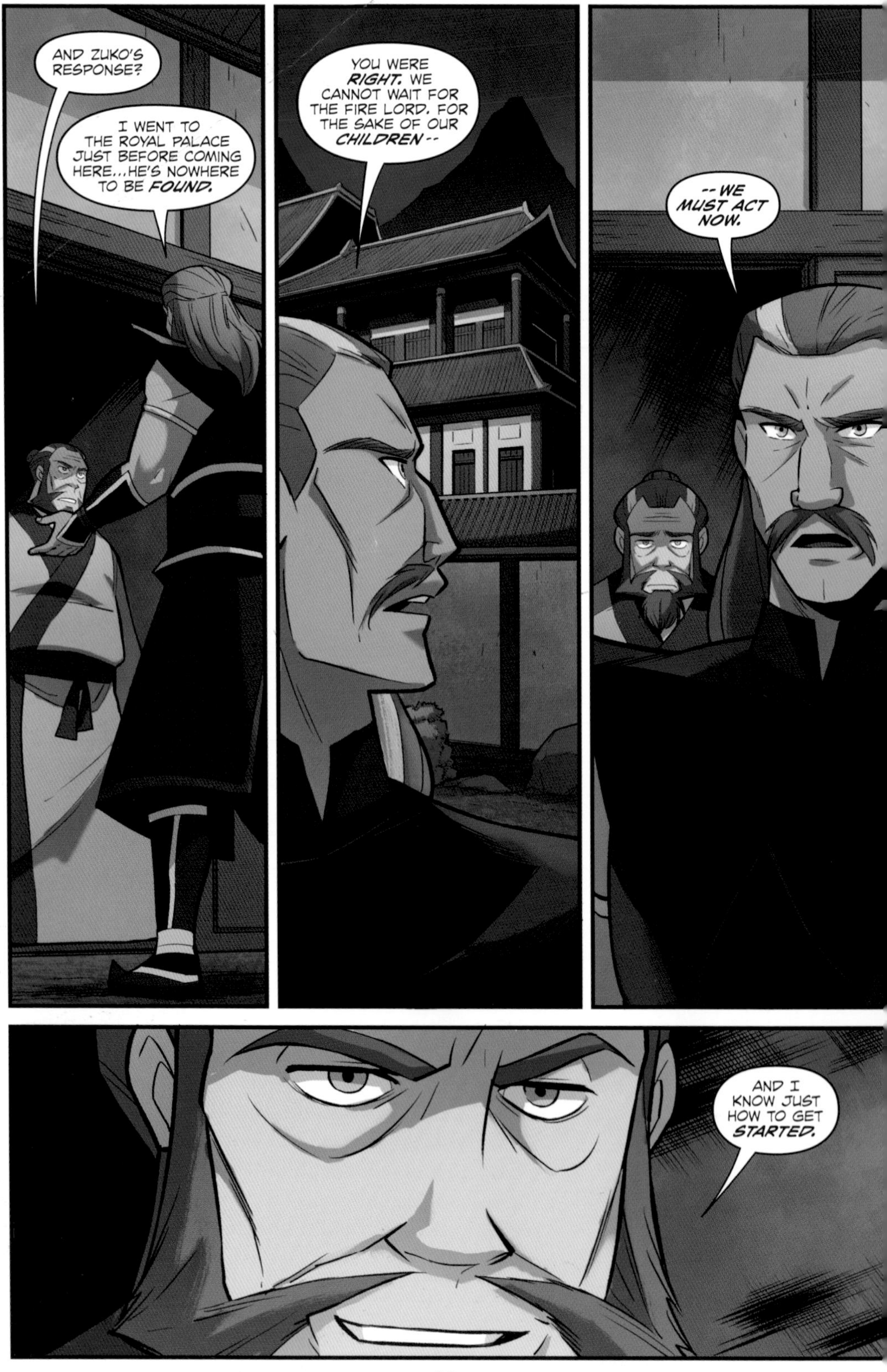
AND ZUKO'S RESPONSE?
I WENT TO THE ROYAL PALACE JUST BEFORE COMING HERE...HE'S NOWHERE TO BE FOUND.
YOU WERE RIGHT. WE CANNOT WAIT FOR THE FIRE LORD. FOR THE SAKE OF OUR CHILDREN --
-- WE MUST ACT NOW.
AND I KNOW JUST HOW TO GET STARTED.

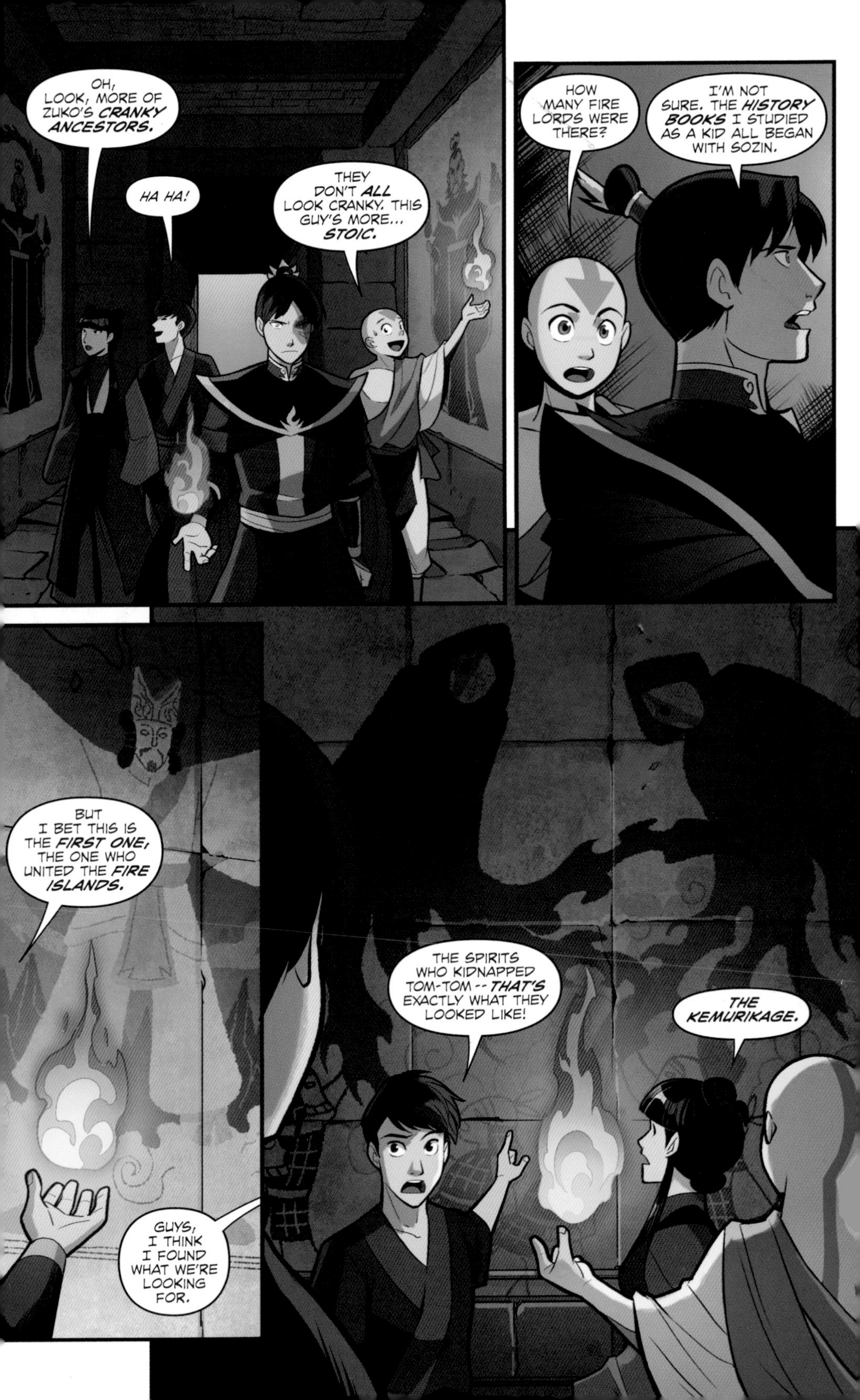
OH, LOOK, MORE OF ZUKO'S CRANKY ANCESTORS.
HA HA!
THEY DON'T ALL LOOK CRANKY. THIS GUY'S MORE... STOIC.
HOW MANY FIRE LORDS WERE THERE?
I'M NOT SURE. THE HISTORY BOOKS I STUDIED AS A KID ALL BEGAN WITH SOZIN.
BUT I BET THIS IS THE FIRST ONE, THE ONE WHO UNITED THE FIRE ISLANDS.
GUYS, I THINK I FOUND WHAT WE'RE LOOKING FOR.
THE SPIRITS WHO KIDNAPPED TOM-TOM -- THAT'S EXACTLY WHAT THEY LOOKED LIKE!
THE KEMURIKAGE.

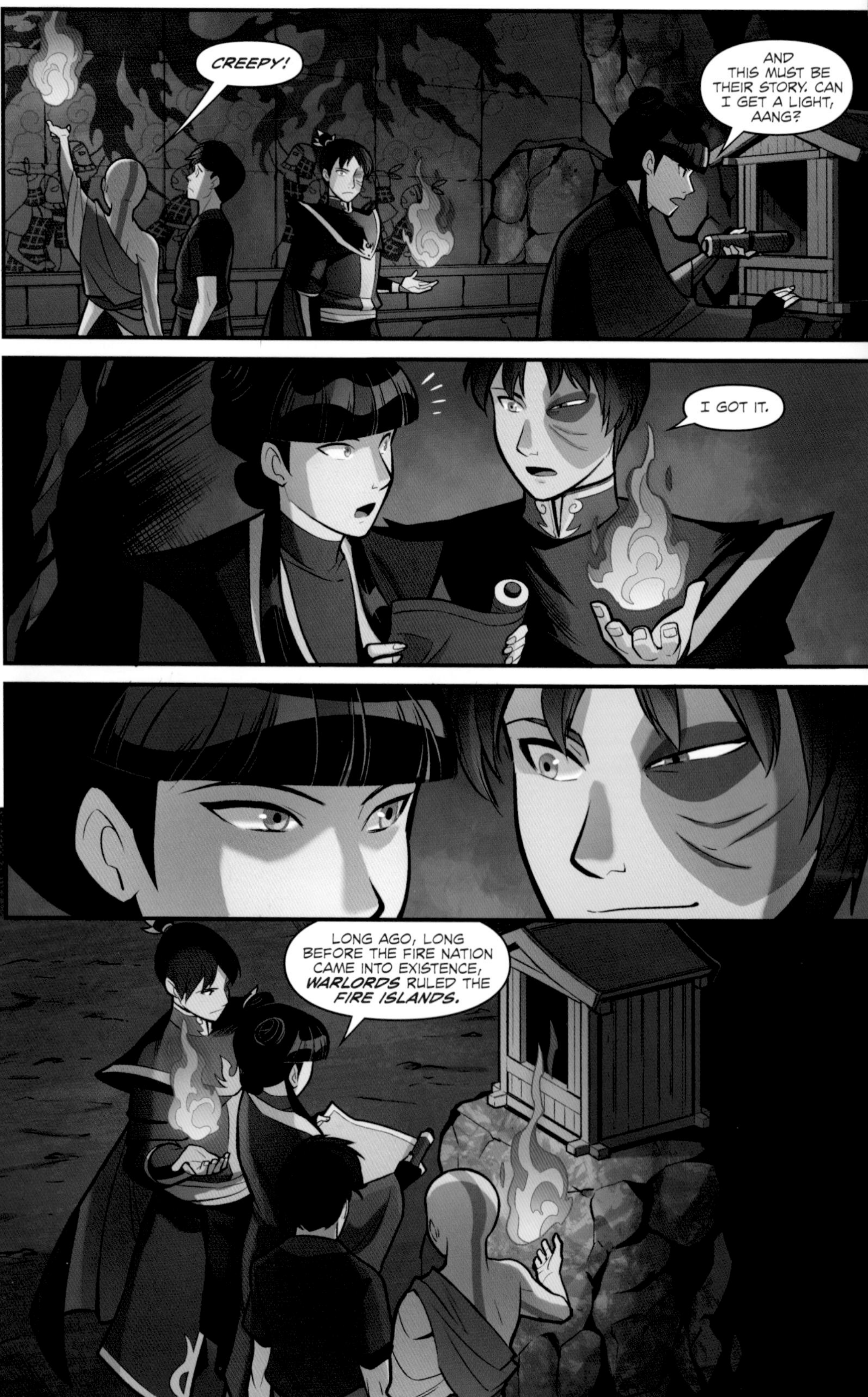
CREEPY!
AND THIS MUST BE THEIR STORY. CAN I GET A LIGHT, AANG?
I GOT IT.
LONG AGO, LONG BEFORE THE FIRE NATION CAME INTO EXISTENCE, **WARLORDS** RULED THE ***FIRE ISLANDS.***

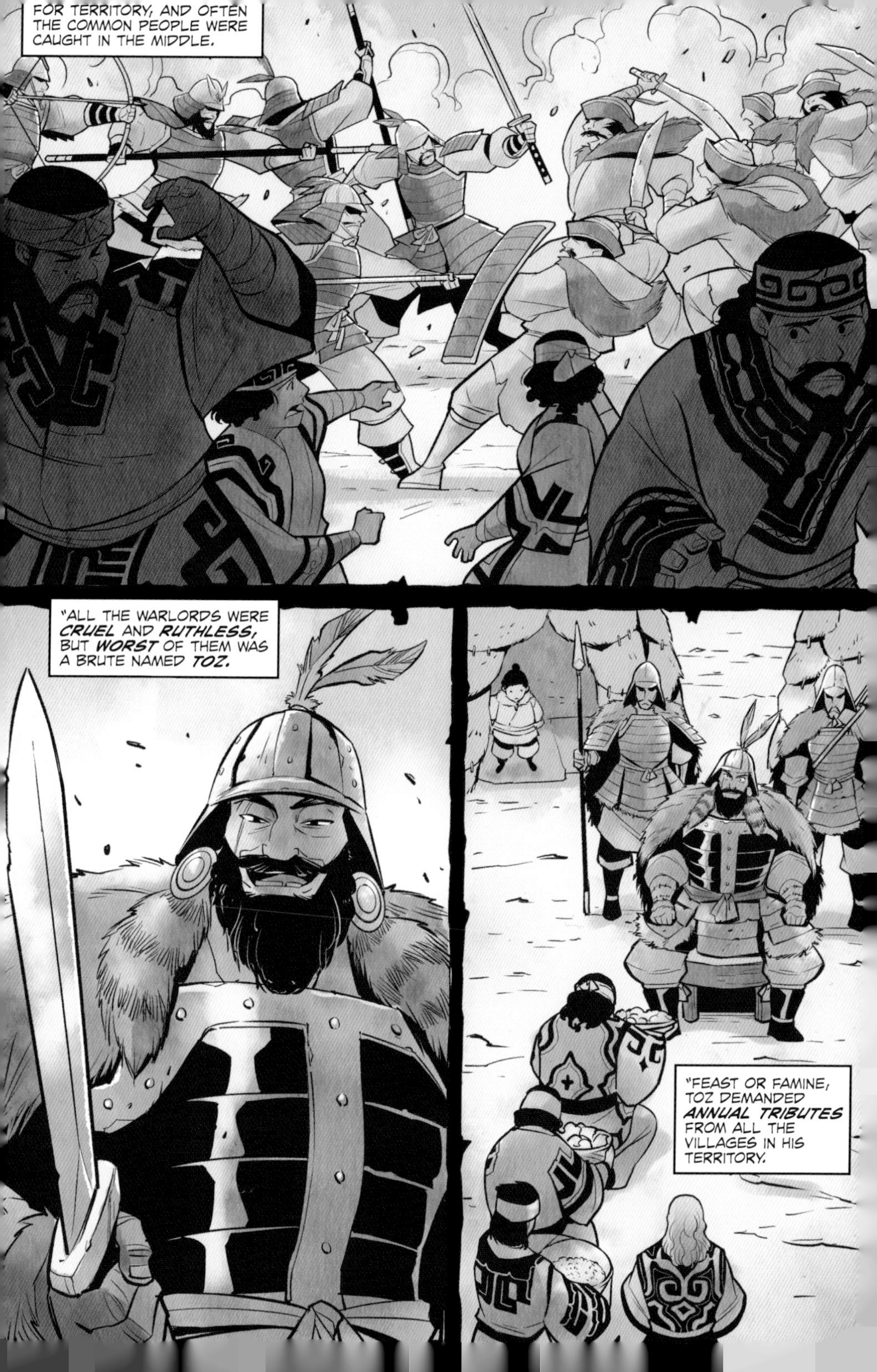
FOR TERRITORY, AND OFTEN THE COMMON PEOPLE WERE CAUGHT IN THE MIDDLE.
"ALL THE WARLORDS WERE CRUEL AND RUTHLESS, BUT WORST OF THEM WAS A BRUTE NAMED TOZ.
"FEAST OR FAMINE, TOZ DEMANDED ANNUAL TRIBUTES FROM ALL THE VILLAGES IN HIS TERRITORY.

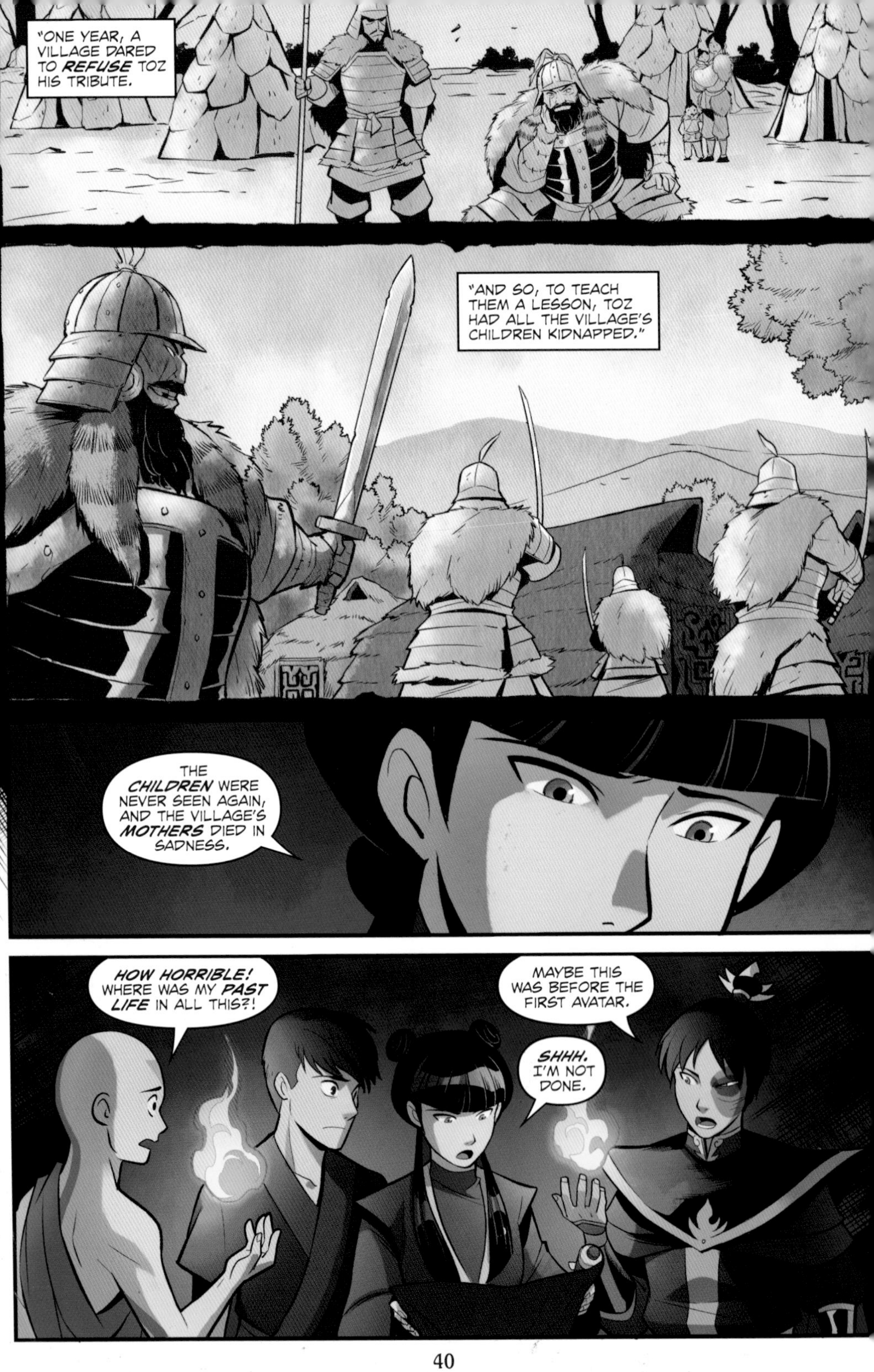
"ONE YEAR, A VILLAGE DARED TO REFUSE TOZ HIS TRIBUTE.
"AND SO, TO TEACH THEM A LESSON, TOZ HAD ALL THE VILLAGE'S CHILDREN KIDNAPPED."
THE CHILDREN WERE NEVER SEEN AGAIN, AND THE VILLAGE'S MOTHERS DIED IN SADNESS.
HOW HORRIBLE! WHERE WAS MY PAST LIFE IN ALL THIS?!
MAYBE THIS WAS BEFORE THE FIRST AVATAR.
SHHH. I'M NOT DONE.

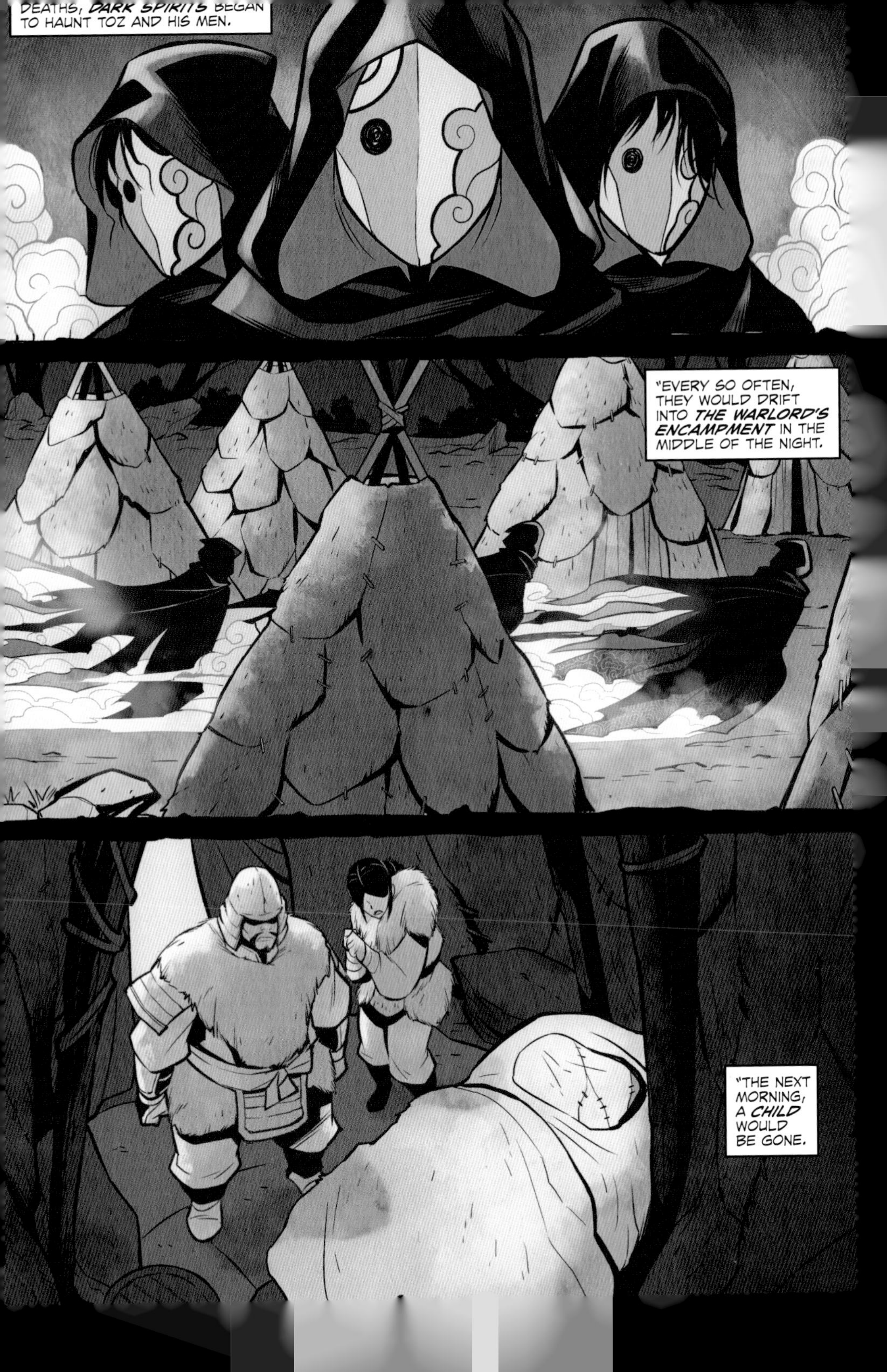
DEATHS, DARK SPIRITS BEGAN TO HAUNT TOZ AND HIS MEN.
"EVERY SO OFTEN, THEY WOULD DRIFT INTO THE WARLORD'S ENCAMPMENT IN THE MIDDLE OF THE NIGHT.
"THE NEXT MORNING, A CHILD WOULD BE GONE.

"OUT OF FEAR, TOZ'S MEN ABANDONED HIM. HIS REGIME *COLLAPSED.*"

HOWEVER, THE DARK SPIRITS--THE *KEMURIKAGE* --CONTINUE TO APPEAR, EVEN TO THIS DAY, THEIR SADNESS *INSATIABLE.*

EEESH. MAYBE SOZIN KEPT ANCIENT FIRE NATION HISTORY LOCKED AWAY BECAUSE IT'S SO *DEPRESSING.*

MAI, I THINK YOU *SUMMONED* SOMETHING BY READING THAT SCROLL!

LOOK!

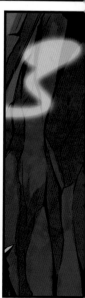

42

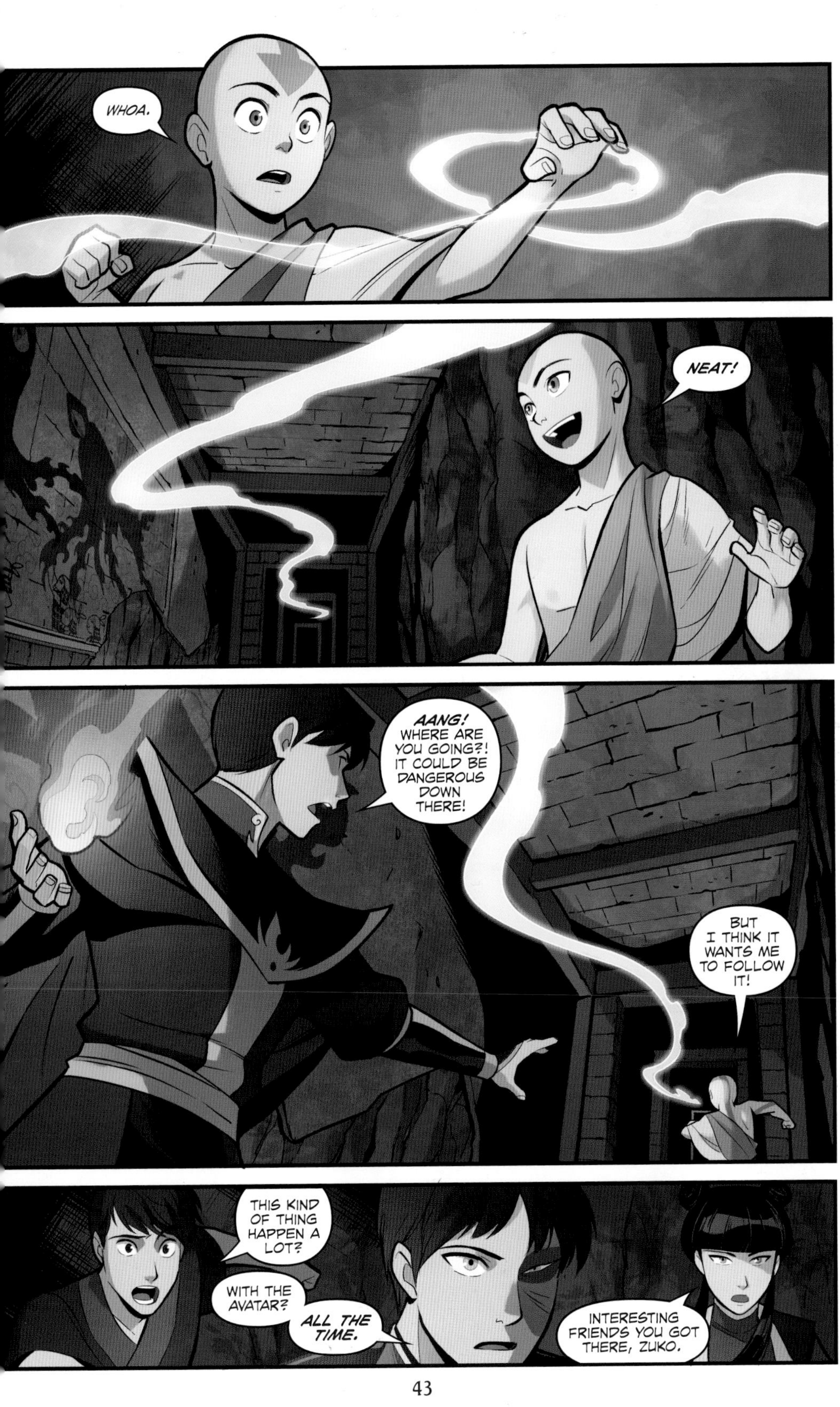
WHOA.
NEAT!
AANG! WHERE ARE YOU GOING?! IT COULD BE DANGEROUS DOWN THERE!
BUT I THINK IT WANTS ME TO FOLLOW IT!
THIS KIND OF THING HAPPEN A LOT?
WITH THE AVATAR?
ALL THE TIME.
INTERESTING FRIENDS YOU GOT THERE, ZUKO.

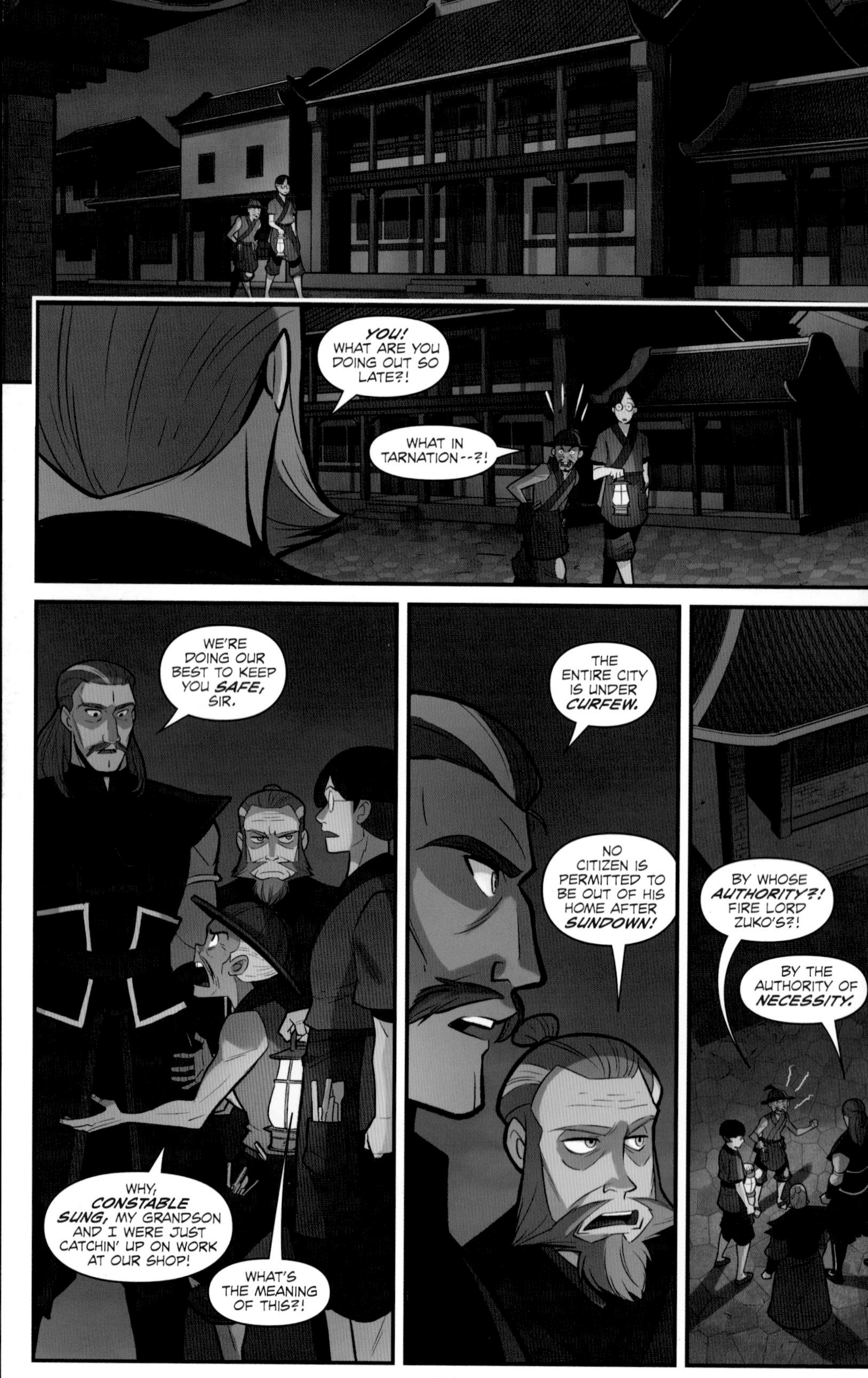
YOU! WHAT ARE YOU DOING OUT SO LATE?!
WHAT IN TARNATION--?!
WE'RE DOING OUR BEST TO KEEP YOU SAFE, SIR.
WHY, CONSTABLE SUNG, MY GRANDSON AND I WERE JUST CATCHIN' UP ON WORK AT OUR SHOP!
WHAT'S THE MEANING OF THIS?!
THE ENTIRE CITY IS UNDER CURFEW.
NO CITIZEN IS PERMITTED TO BE OUT OF HIS HOME AFTER SUNDOWN!
BY WHOSE AUTHORITY?! FIRE LORD ZUKO'S?!
BY THE AUTHORITY OF NECESSITY.

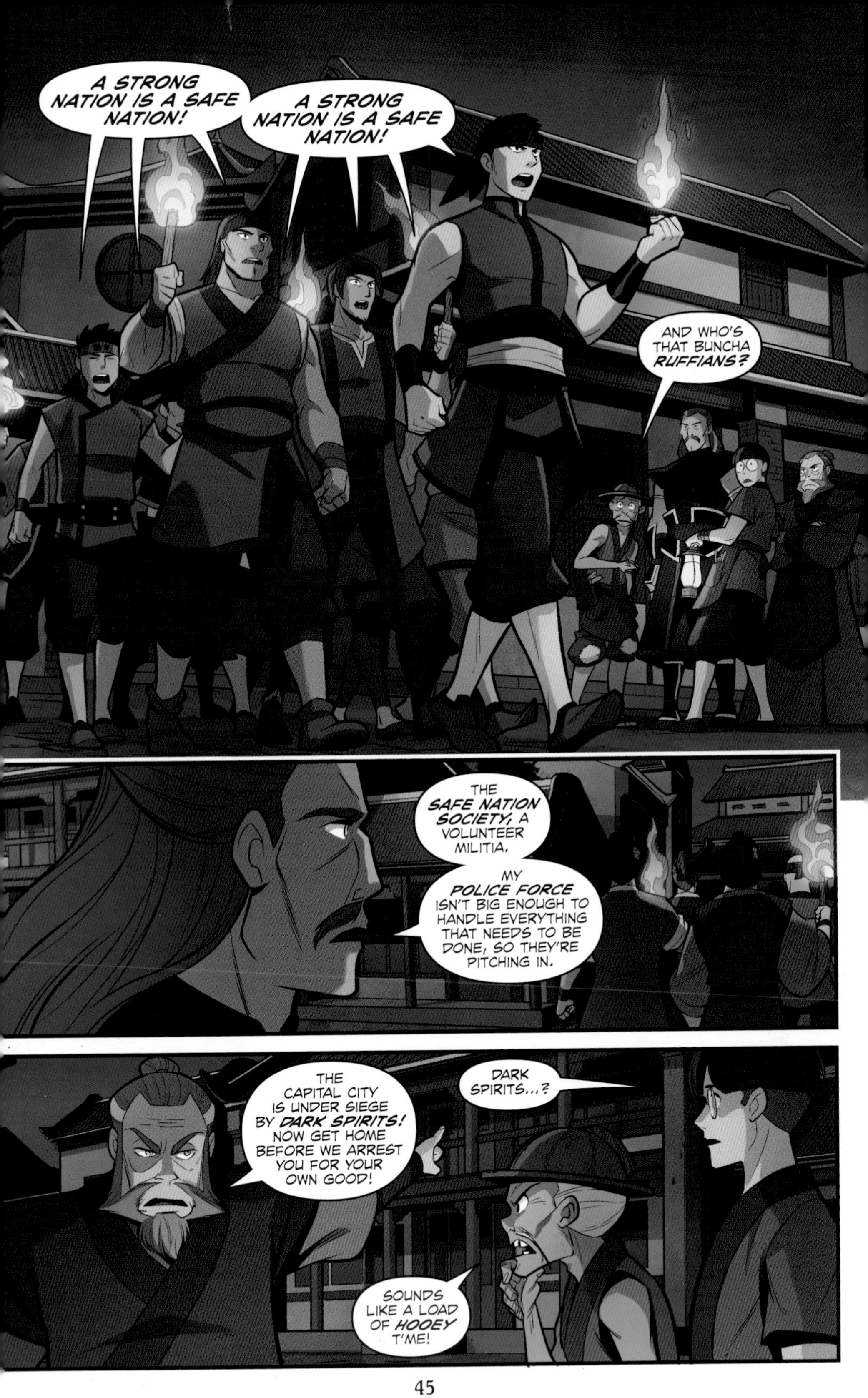
A STRONG NATION IS A SAFE NATION!
A STRONG NATION IS A SAFE NATION!
AND WHO'S THAT BUNCHA RUFFIANS?
THE SAFE NATION SOCIETY; A VOLUNTEER MILITIA.
MY POLICE FORCE ISN'T BIG ENOUGH TO HANDLE EVERYTHING THAT NEEDS TO BE DONE; SO THEY'RE PITCHING IN.
THE CAPITAL CITY IS UNDER SIEGE BY DARK SPIRITS! NOW GET HOME BEFORE WE ARREST YOU FOR YOUR OWN GOOD!
DARK SPIRITS...?
SOUNDS LIKE A LOAD OF HOOEY T'ME!

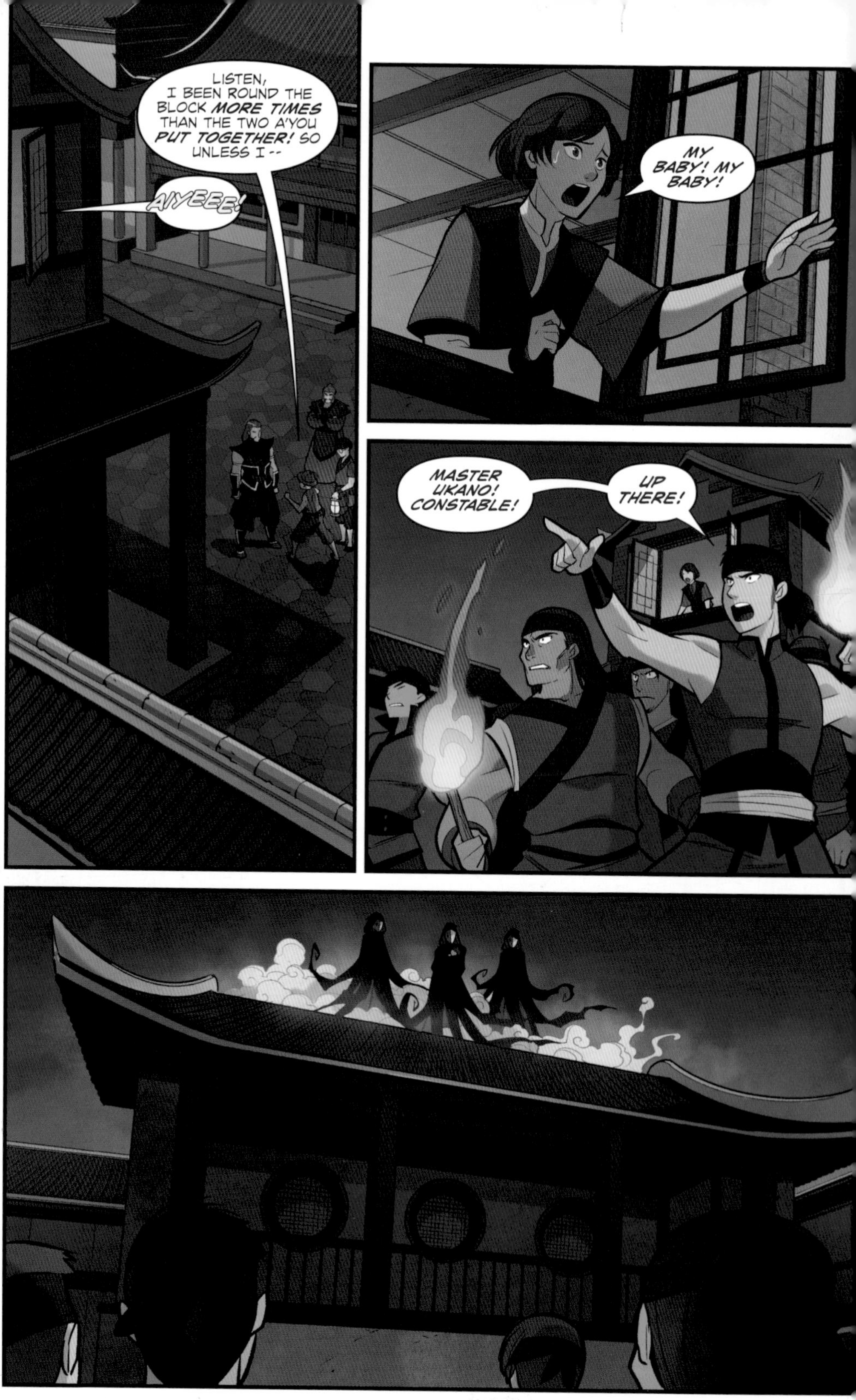
LISTEN, I BEEN ROUND THE BLOCK MORE TIMES THAN THE TWO A'YOU PUT TOGETHER! SO UNLESS I --
AIYEEE!
MY BABY! MY BABY!
MASTER UKANO! CONSTABLE!
UP THERE!

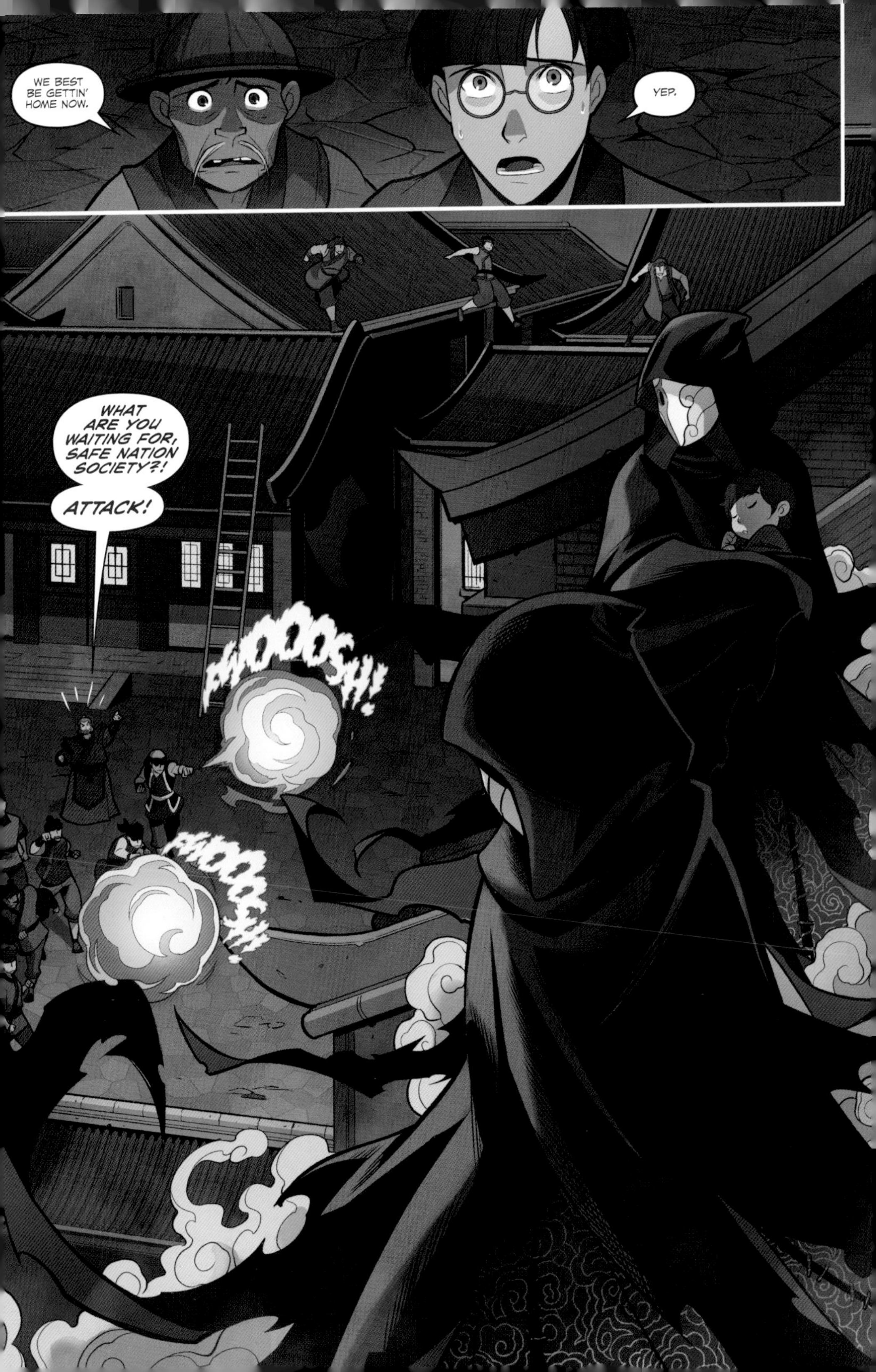
WE BEST BE GETTIN' HOME NOW.
YEP.
WHAT ARE YOU WAITING FOR, SAFE NATION SOCIETY?!
ATTACK!
FWOOOSH!
FWOOOSH!

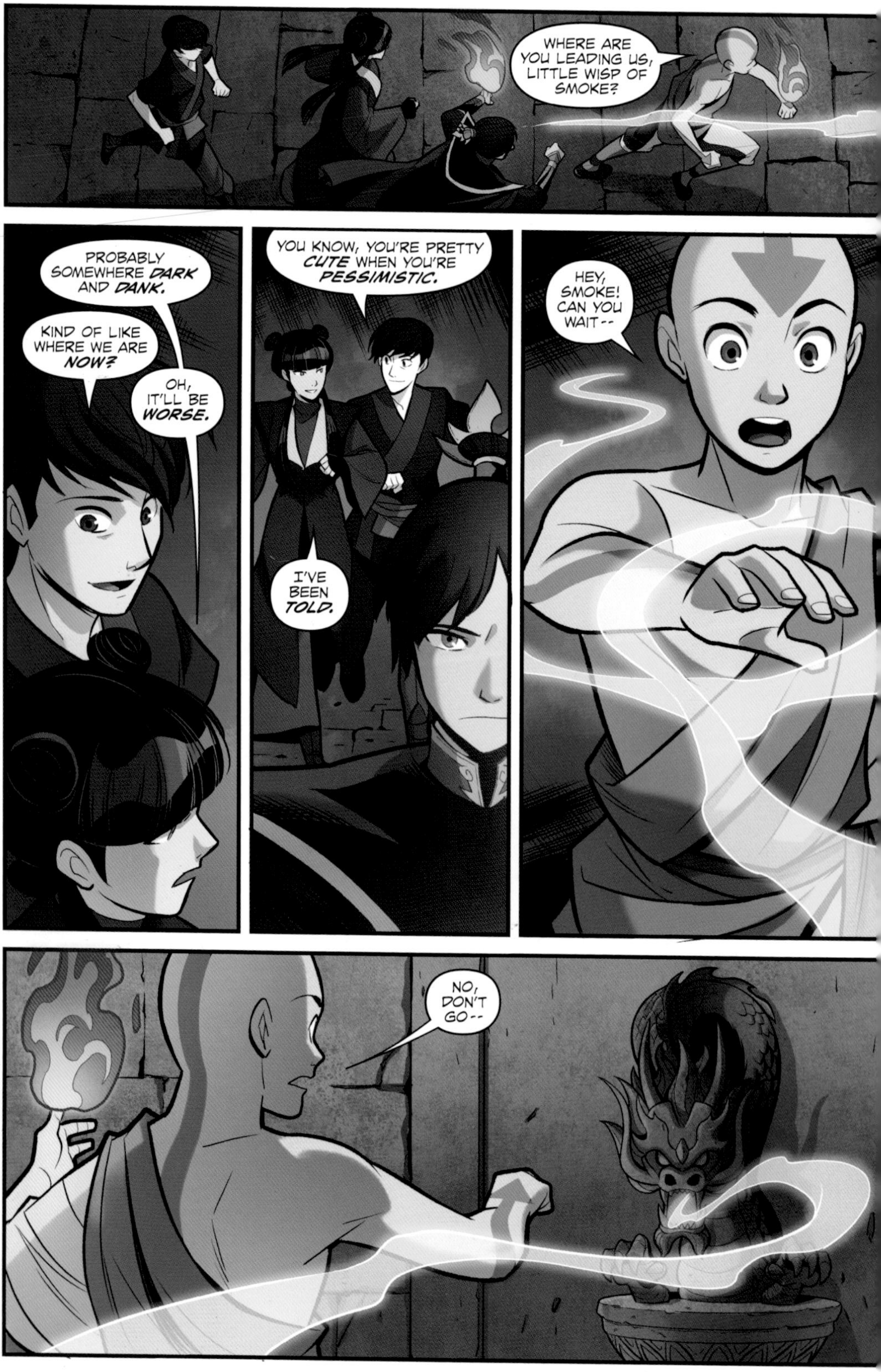
WHERE ARE YOU LEADING US, LITTLE WISP OF SMOKE?
PROBABLY SOMEWHERE DARK AND DANK.
KIND OF LIKE WHERE WE ARE NOW?
OH, IT'LL BE WORSE.
YOU KNOW, YOU'RE PRETTY CUTE WHEN YOU'RE PESSIMISTIC.
I'VE BEEN TOLD.
HEY, SMOKE! CAN YOU WAIT--
NO, DON'T GO--

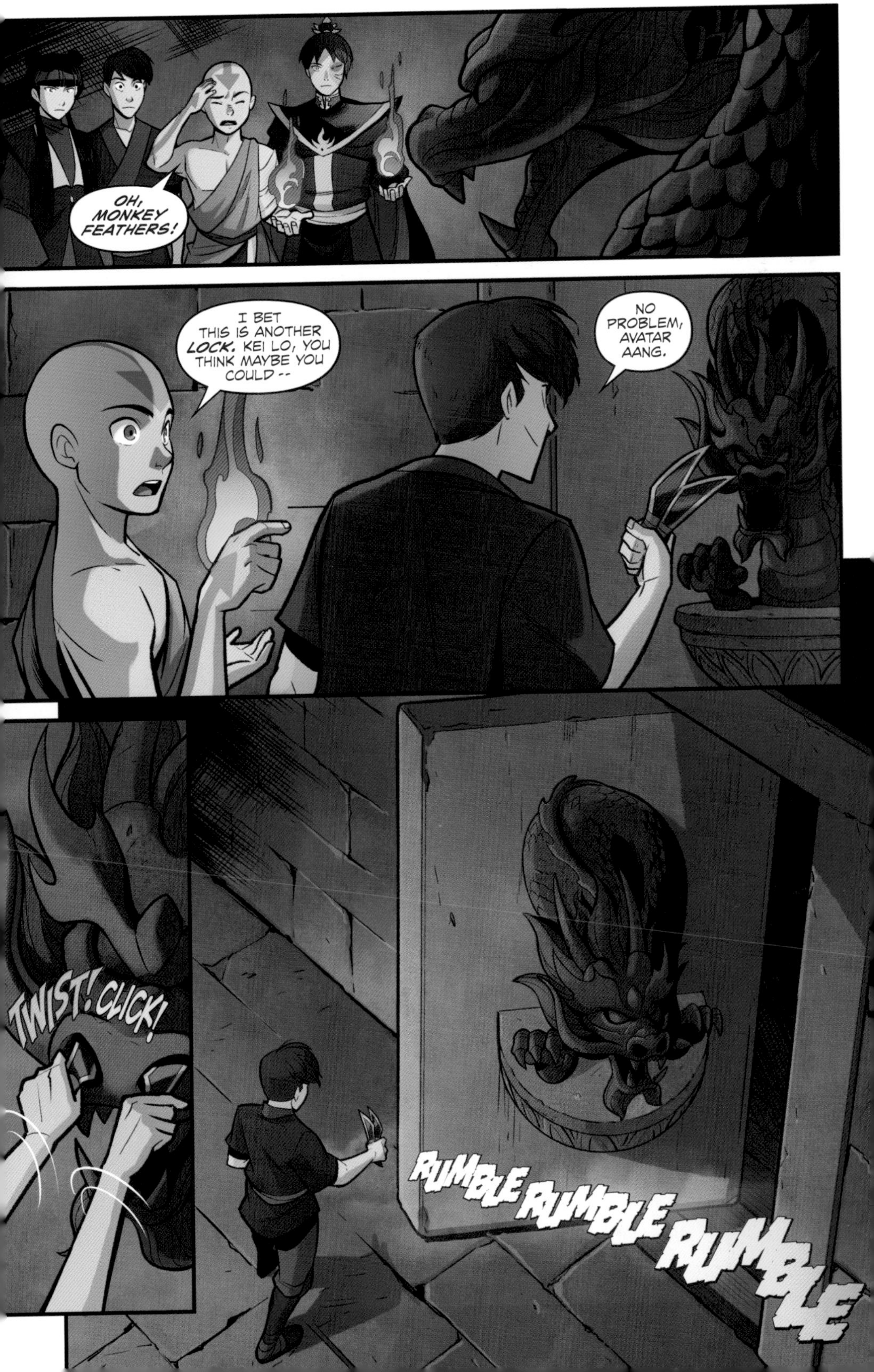
OH, MONKEY FEATHERS!
I BET THIS IS ANOTHER LOCK. KEI LO, YOU THINK MAYBE YOU COULD --
NO PROBLEM, AVATAR AANG.
TWIST! CLICK!
RUMBLE RUMBLE RUMBLE

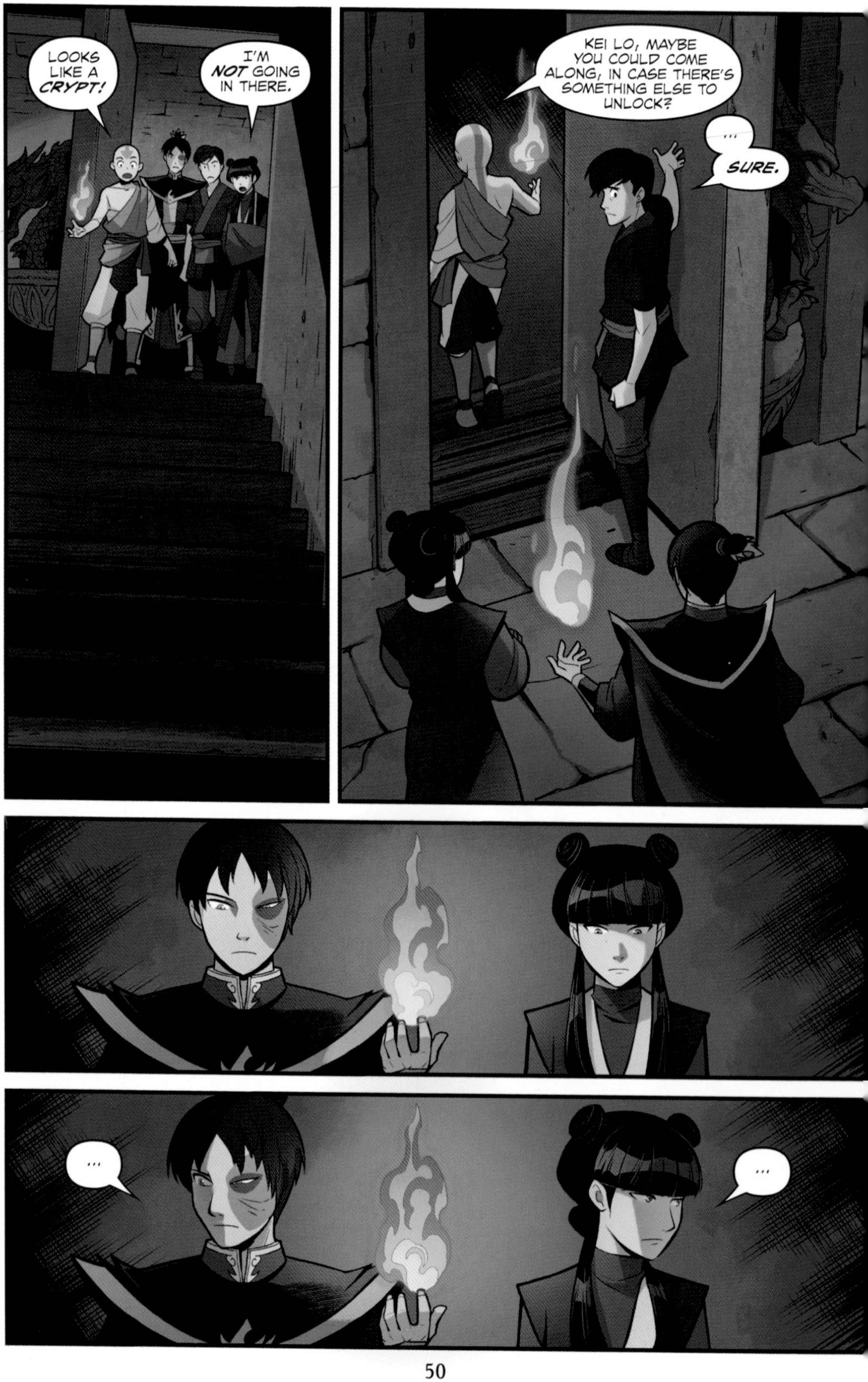
LOOKS LIKE A *CRYPT!*
I'M *NOT* GOING IN THERE.
KEI LO, MAYBE YOU COULD COME ALONG, IN CASE THERE'S SOMETHING ELSE TO UNLOCK?
...
SURE.
...
...

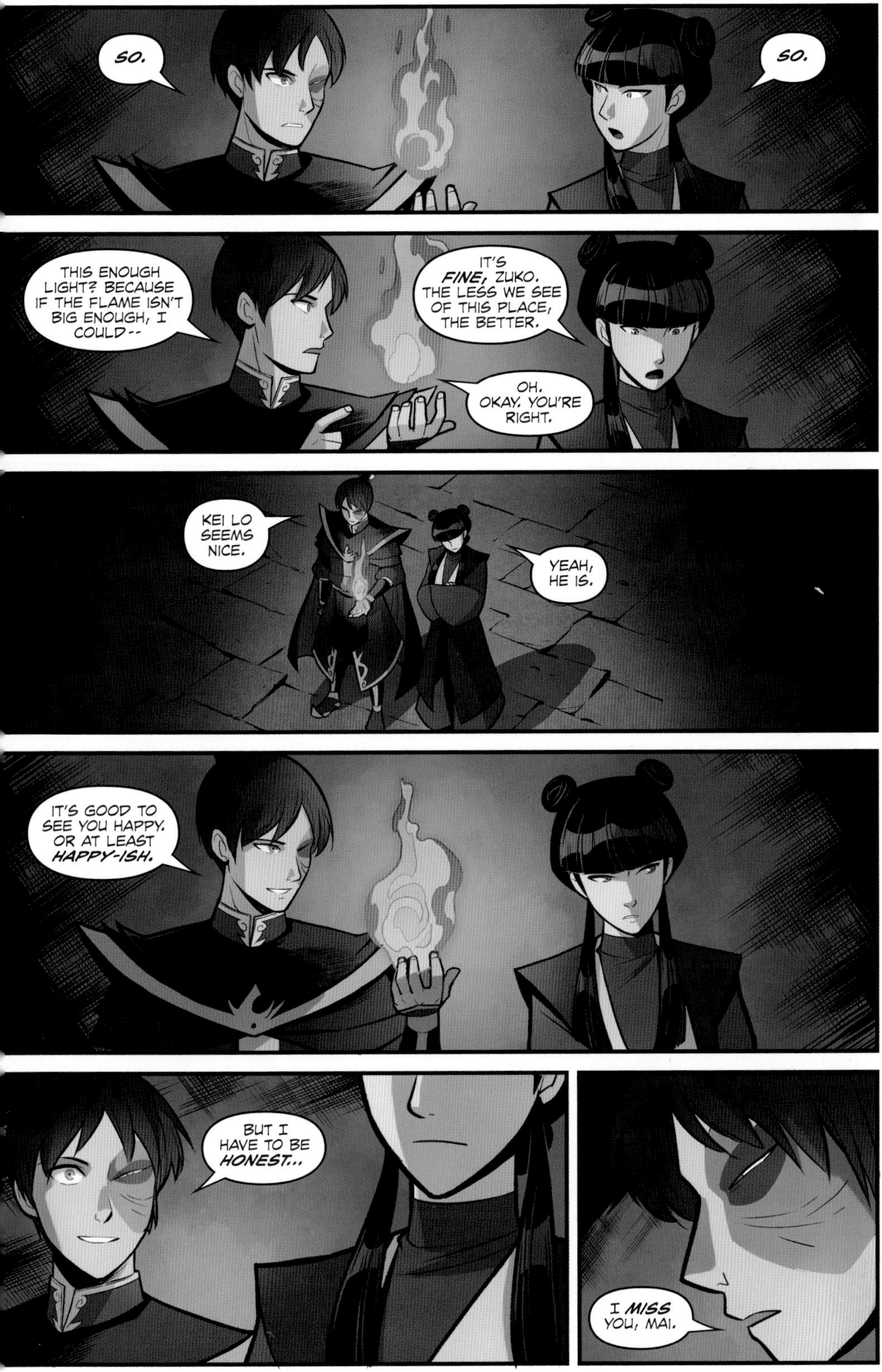
SO.
SO.
THIS ENOUGH LIGHT? BECAUSE IF THE FLAME ISN'T BIG ENOUGH, I COULD--
IT'S FINE, ZUKO. THE LESS WE SEE OF THIS PLACE, THE BETTER.
OH. OKAY. YOU'RE RIGHT.
KEI LO SEEMS NICE.
YEAH, HE IS.
IT'S GOOD TO SEE YOU HAPPY. OR AT LEAST HAPPY-ISH.
BUT I HAVE TO BE HONEST...
I MISS YOU, MAI.

UGH! WHY WOULD YOU SAY SOMETHING LIKE THAT?!

BECAUSE IT'S *TRUE!*

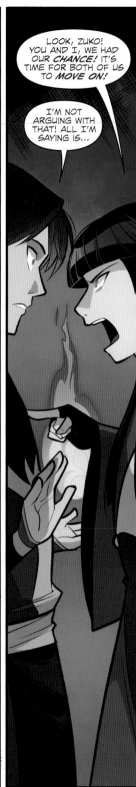

LOOK, ZUKO! YOU AND I, WE HAD OUR *CHANCE!* IT'S TIME FOR BOTH OF US TO *MOVE ON!*

I'M NOT ARGUING WITH THAT! ALL I'M SAYING IS...

I DON'T KNOW WHAT I'M SAYING.

STOP.

TELL ME, DO YOU FEEL ABOUT *HIM* THE SAME WAY YOU USED TO FEEL ABOUT *ME?*

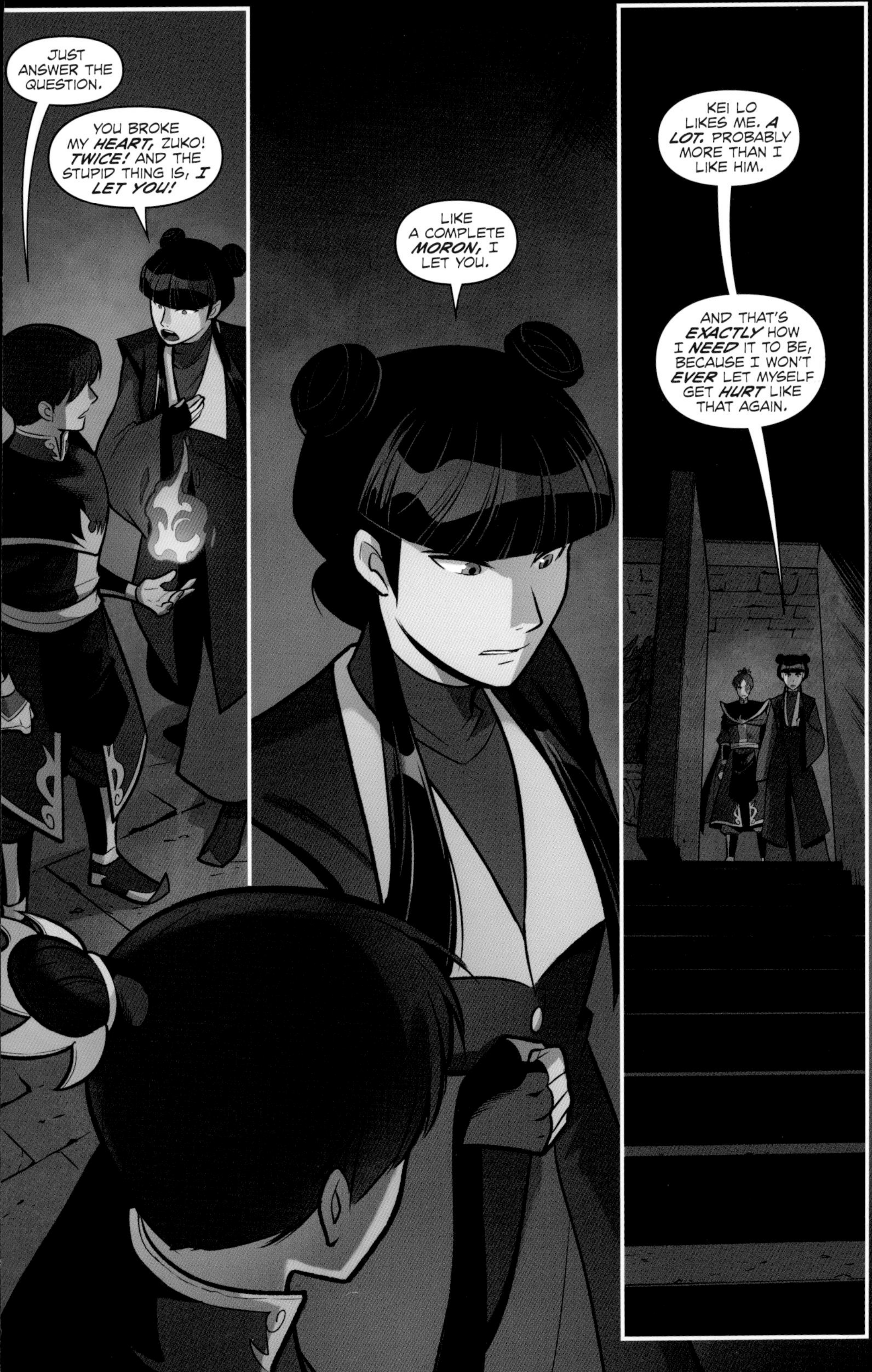
JUST ANSWER THE QUESTION.
YOU BROKE MY HEART, ZUKO! TWICE! AND THE STUPID THING IS, I LET YOU!
LIKE A COMPLETE MORON, I LET YOU.
KEI LO LIKES ME. A LOT. PROBABLY MORE THAN I LIKE HIM.
AND THAT'S EXACTLY HOW I NEED IT TO BE, BECAUSE I WON'T EVER LET MYSELF GET HURT LIKE THAT AGAIN.

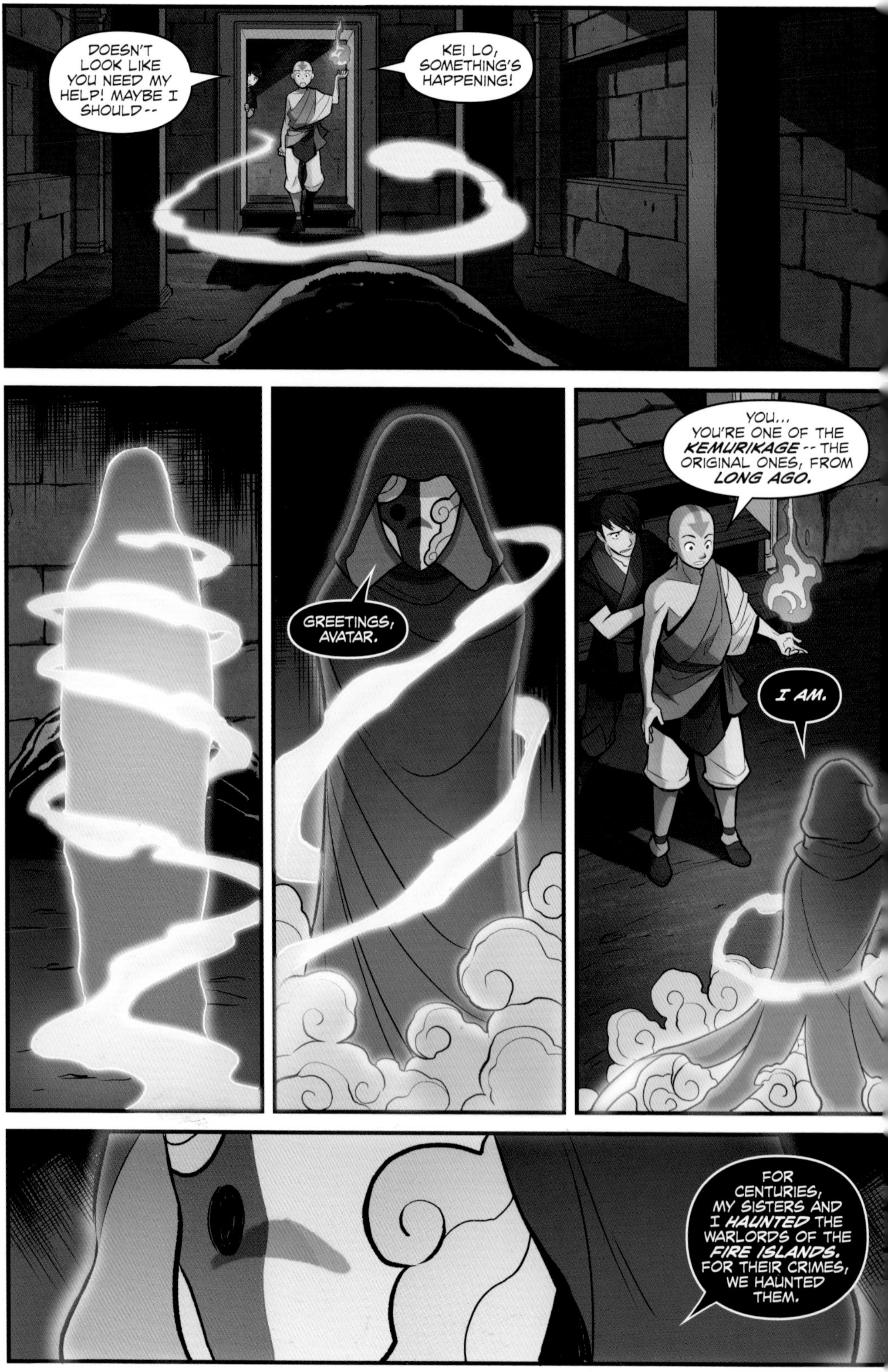
DOESN'T LOOK LIKE YOU NEED MY HELP! MAYBE I SHOULD--
KEI LO, SOMETHING'S HAPPENING!
GREETINGS, AVATAR.
YOU... YOU'RE ONE OF THE KEMURIKAGE -- THE ORIGINAL ONES, FROM LONG AGO.
I AM.
FOR CENTURIES, MY SISTERS AND I HAUNTED THE WARLORDS OF THE FIRE ISLANDS. FOR THEIR CRIMES, WE HAUNTED THEM.

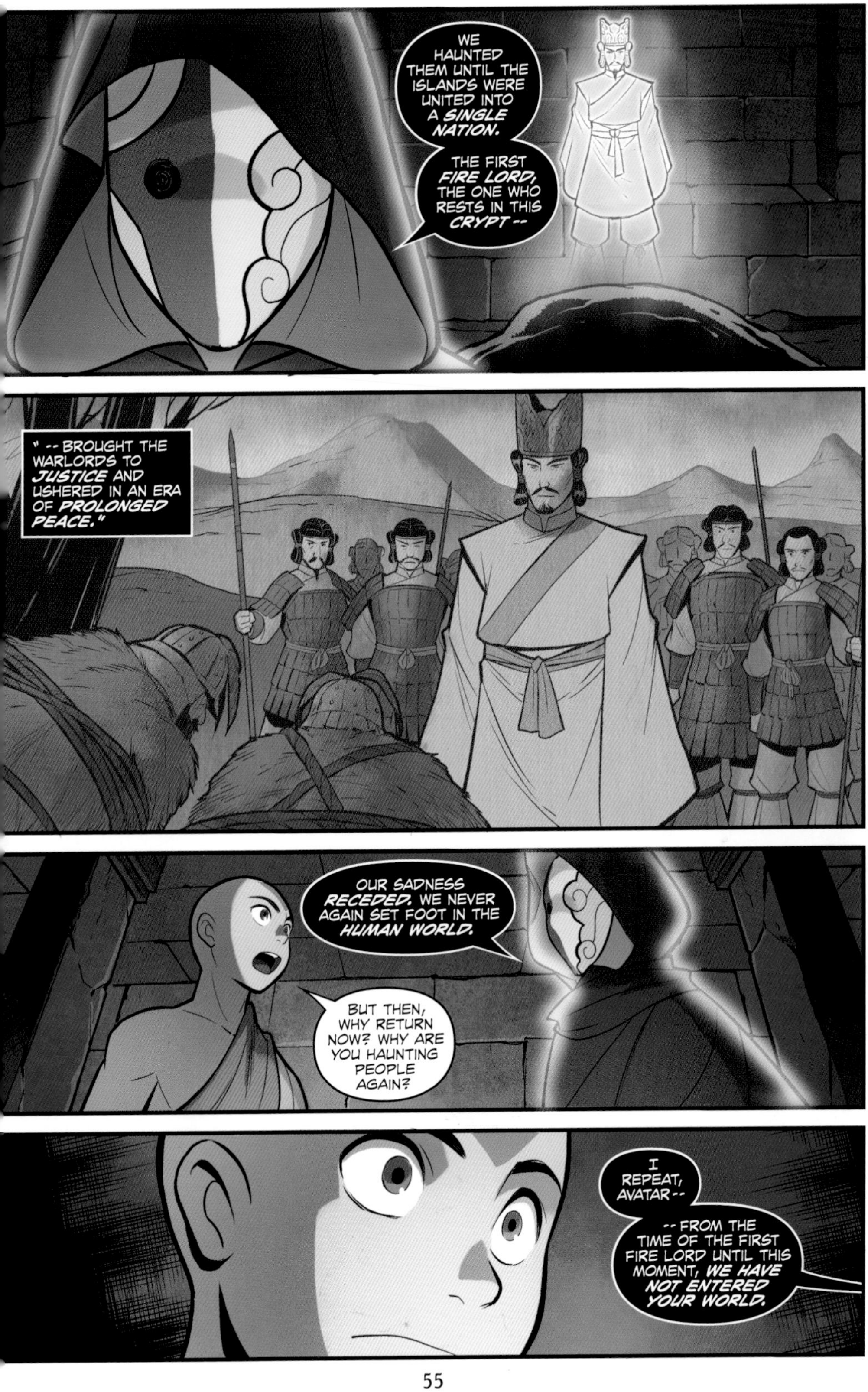
WE HAUNTED THEM UNTIL THE ISLANDS WERE UNITED INTO A SINGLE NATION.
THE FIRST FIRE LORD, THE ONE WHO RESTS IN THIS CRYPT --
" -- BROUGHT THE WARLORDS TO JUSTICE AND USHERED IN AN ERA OF PROLONGED PEACE."
OUR SADNESS RECEDED. WE NEVER AGAIN SET FOOT IN THE HUMAN WORLD.
BUT THEN, WHY RETURN NOW? WHY ARE YOU HAUNTING PEOPLE AGAIN?
I REPEAT, AVATAR --
-- FROM THE TIME OF THE FIRST FIRE LORD UNTIL THIS MOMENT, WE HAVE NOT ENTERED YOUR WORLD.

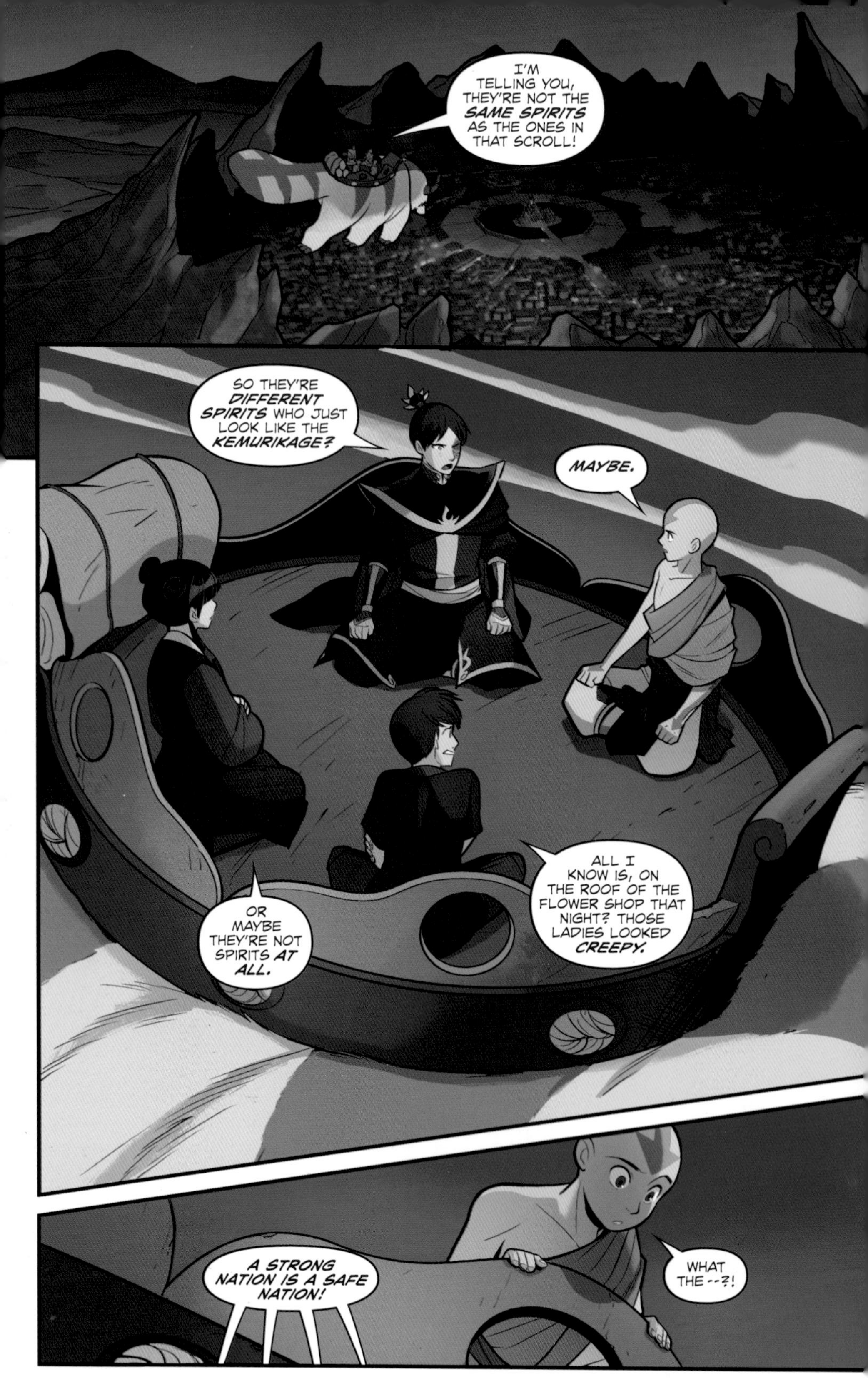
I'M TELLING YOU, THEY'RE NOT THE SAME SPIRITS AS THE ONES IN THAT SCROLL!
SO THEY'RE DIFFERENT SPIRITS WHO JUST LOOK LIKE THE KEMURIKAGE?
MAYBE.
OR MAYBE THEY'RE NOT SPIRITS AT ALL.
ALL I KNOW IS, ON THE ROOF OF THE FLOWER SHOP THAT NIGHT? THOSE LADIES LOOKED CREEPY.
A STRONG NATION IS A SAFE NATION!
WHAT THE--?!

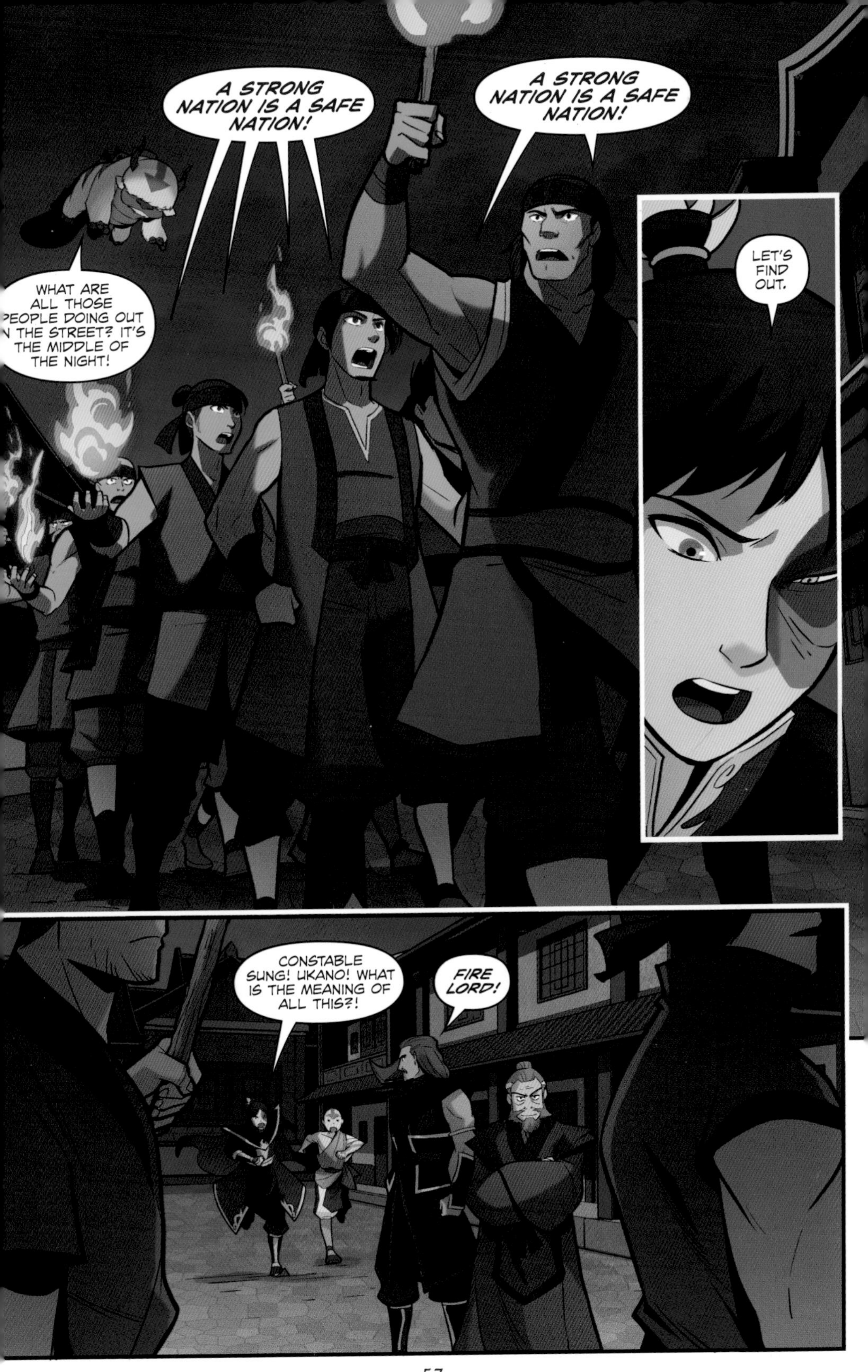
A STRONG NATION IS A SAFE NATION!
A STRONG NATION IS A SAFE NATION!
WHAT ARE ALL THOSE PEOPLE DOING OUT IN THE STREET? IT'S THE MIDDLE OF THE NIGHT!
LET'S FIND OUT.
CONSTABLE SUNG! UKANO! WHAT IS THE MEANING OF ALL THIS?!
FIRE LORD!

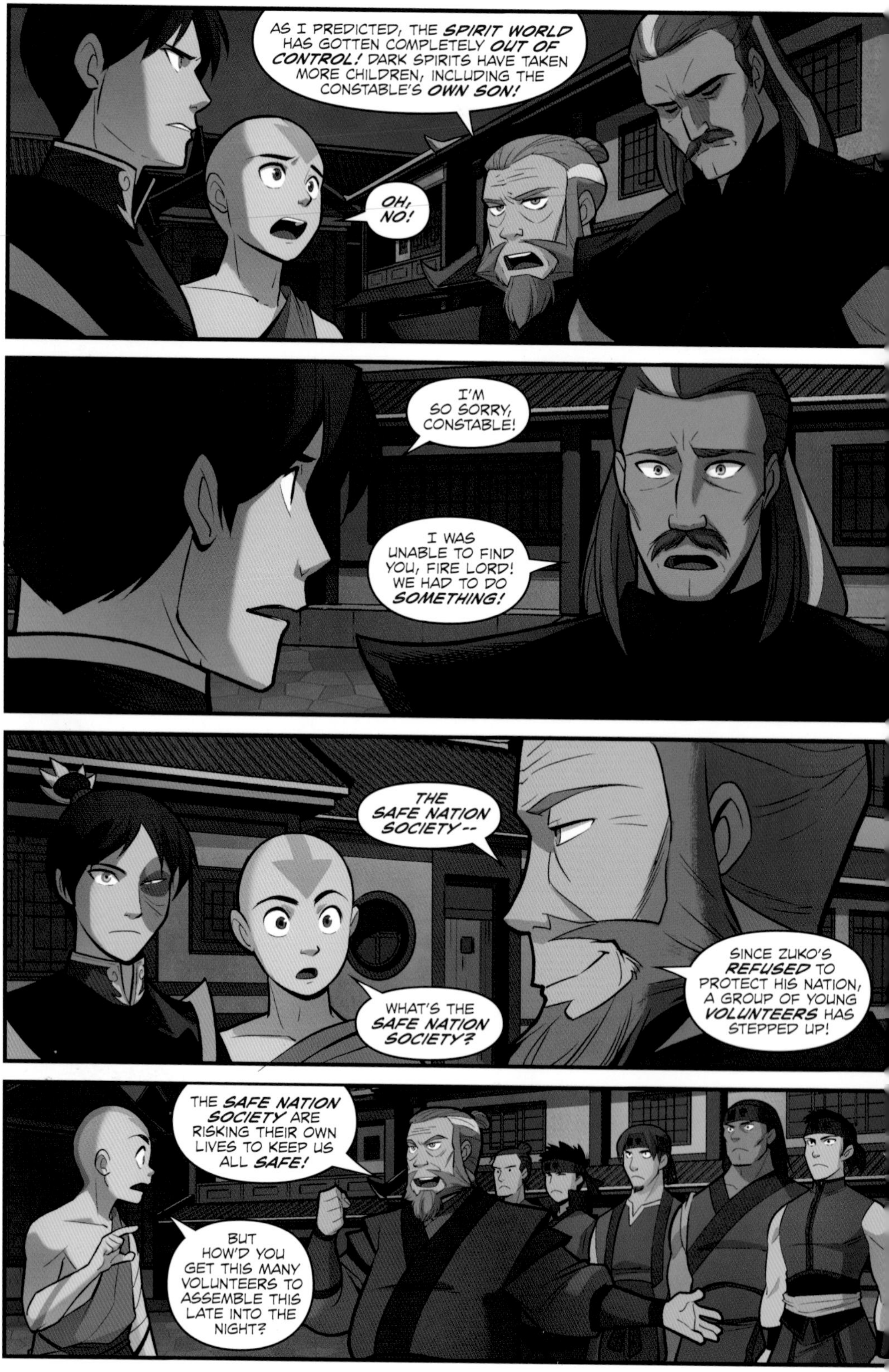
AS I PREDICTED, THE SPIRIT WORLD HAS GOTTEN COMPLETELY OUT OF CONTROL! DARK SPIRITS HAVE TAKEN MORE CHILDREN, INCLUDING THE CONSTABLE'S OWN SON!
OH, NO!
I'M SO SORRY, CONSTABLE!
I WAS UNABLE TO FIND YOU, FIRE LORD! WE HAD TO DO SOMETHING!
THE SAFE NATION SOCIETY--
WHAT'S THE SAFE NATION SOCIETY?
SINCE ZUKO'S REFUSED TO PROTECT HIS NATION, A GROUP OF YOUNG VOLUNTEERS HAS STEPPED UP!
THE SAFE NATION SOCIETY ARE RISKING THEIR OWN LIVES TO KEEP US ALL SAFE!
BUT HOW'D YOU GET THIS MANY VOLUNTEERS TO ASSEMBLE THIS LATE INTO THE NIGHT?

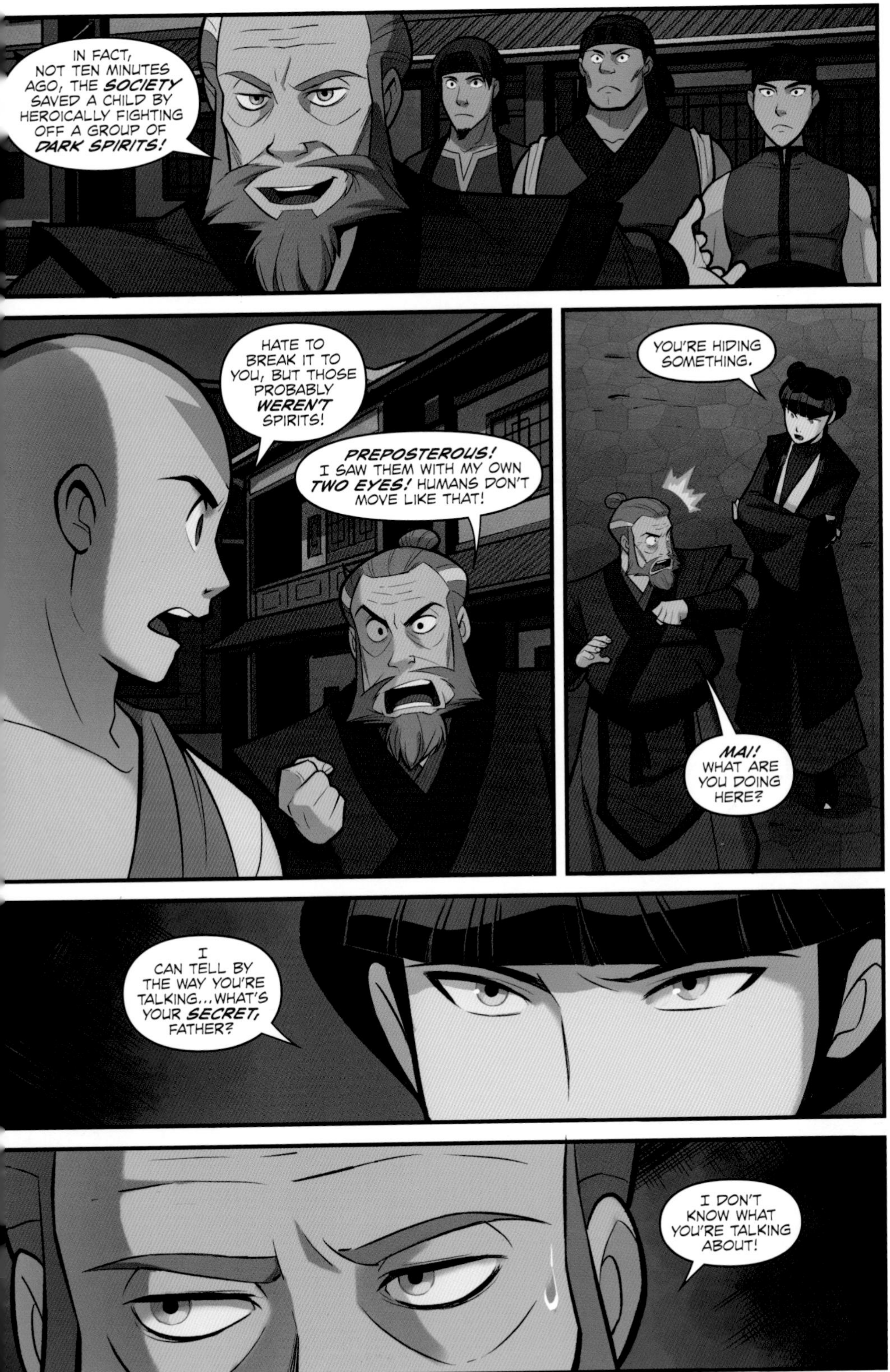
IN FACT, NOT TEN MINUTES AGO, THE SOCIETY SAVED A CHILD BY HEROICALLY FIGHTING OFF A GROUP OF DARK SPIRITS!
HATE TO BREAK IT TO YOU, BUT THOSE PROBABLY WEREN'T SPIRITS!
PREPOSTEROUS! I SAW THEM WITH MY OWN TWO EYES! HUMANS DON'T MOVE LIKE THAT!
YOU'RE HIDING SOMETHING.
MAI! WHAT ARE YOU DOING HERE?
I CAN TELL BY THE WAY YOU'RE TALKING...WHAT'S YOUR SECRET, FATHER?
I DON'T KNOW WHAT YOU'RE TALKING ABOUT!

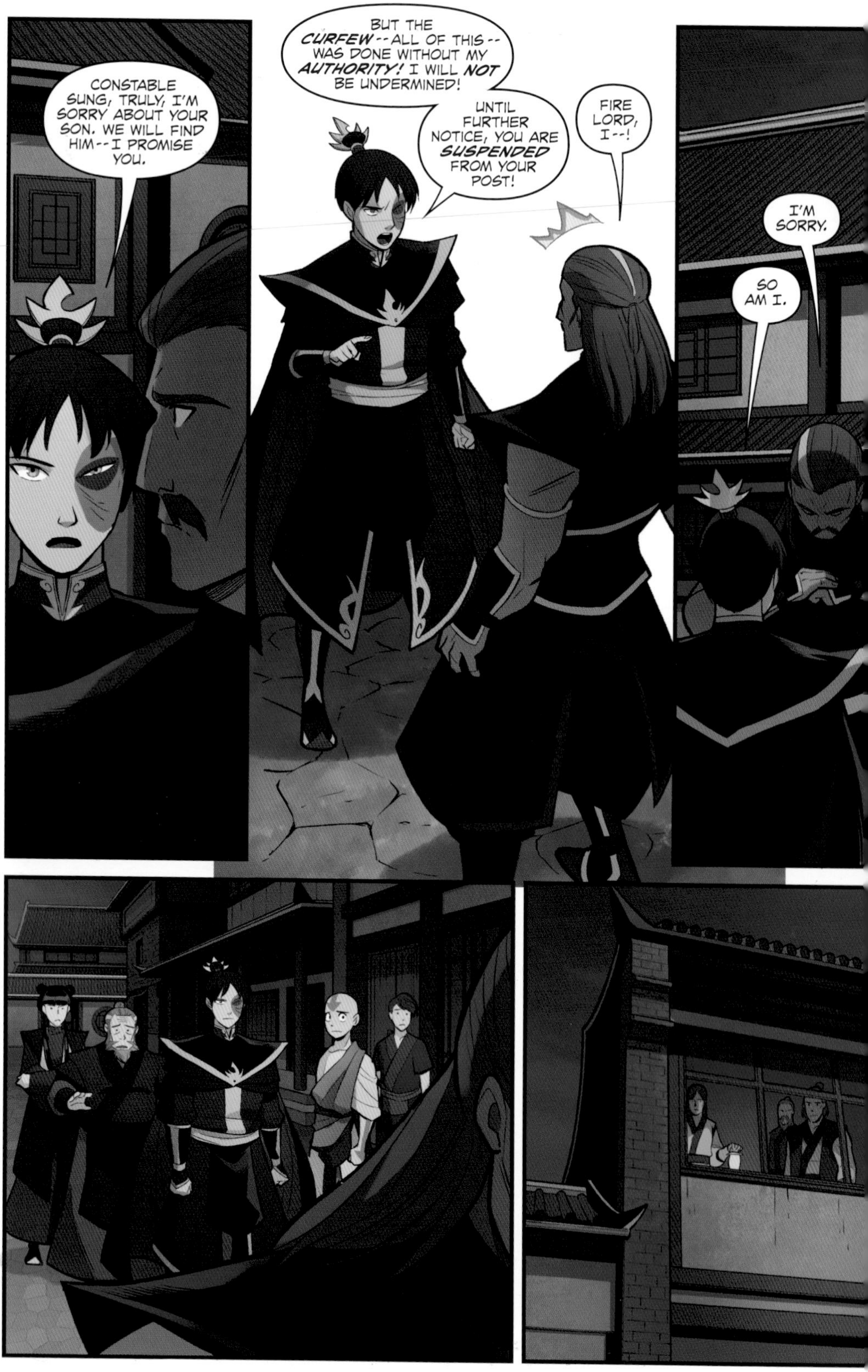
CONSTABLE SUNG, TRULY, I'M SORRY ABOUT YOUR SON. WE WILL FIND HIM--I PROMISE YOU.
BUT THE CURFEW--ALL OF THIS--WAS DONE WITHOUT MY AUTHORITY! I WILL NOT BE UNDERMINED!
UNTIL FURTHER NOTICE, YOU ARE SUSPENDED FROM YOUR POST!
FIRE LORD, I--!
I'M SORRY.
SO AM I.

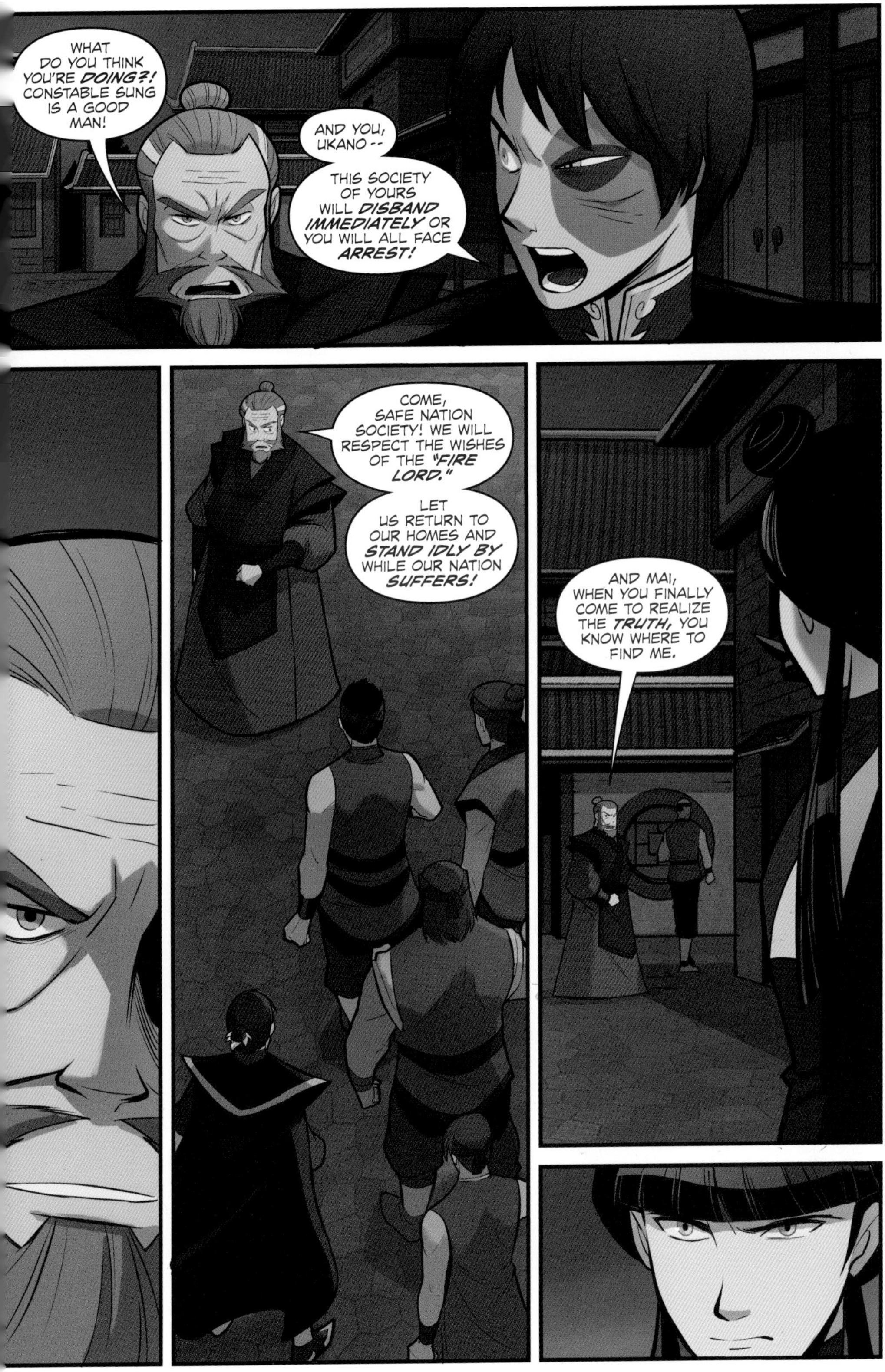

WHAT DO YOU THINK YOU'RE DOING?! CONSTABLE SUNG IS A GOOD MAN!
AND YOU, UKANO --
THIS SOCIETY OF YOURS WILL DISBAND IMMEDIATELY OR YOU WILL ALL FACE ARREST!
COME, SAFE NATION SOCIETY! WE WILL RESPECT THE WISHES OF THE "FIRE LORD."
LET US RETURN TO OUR HOMES AND STAND IDLY BY WHILE OUR NATION SUFFERS!
AND MAI, WHEN YOU FINALLY COME TO REALIZE THE TRUTH, YOU KNOW WHERE TO FIND ME.

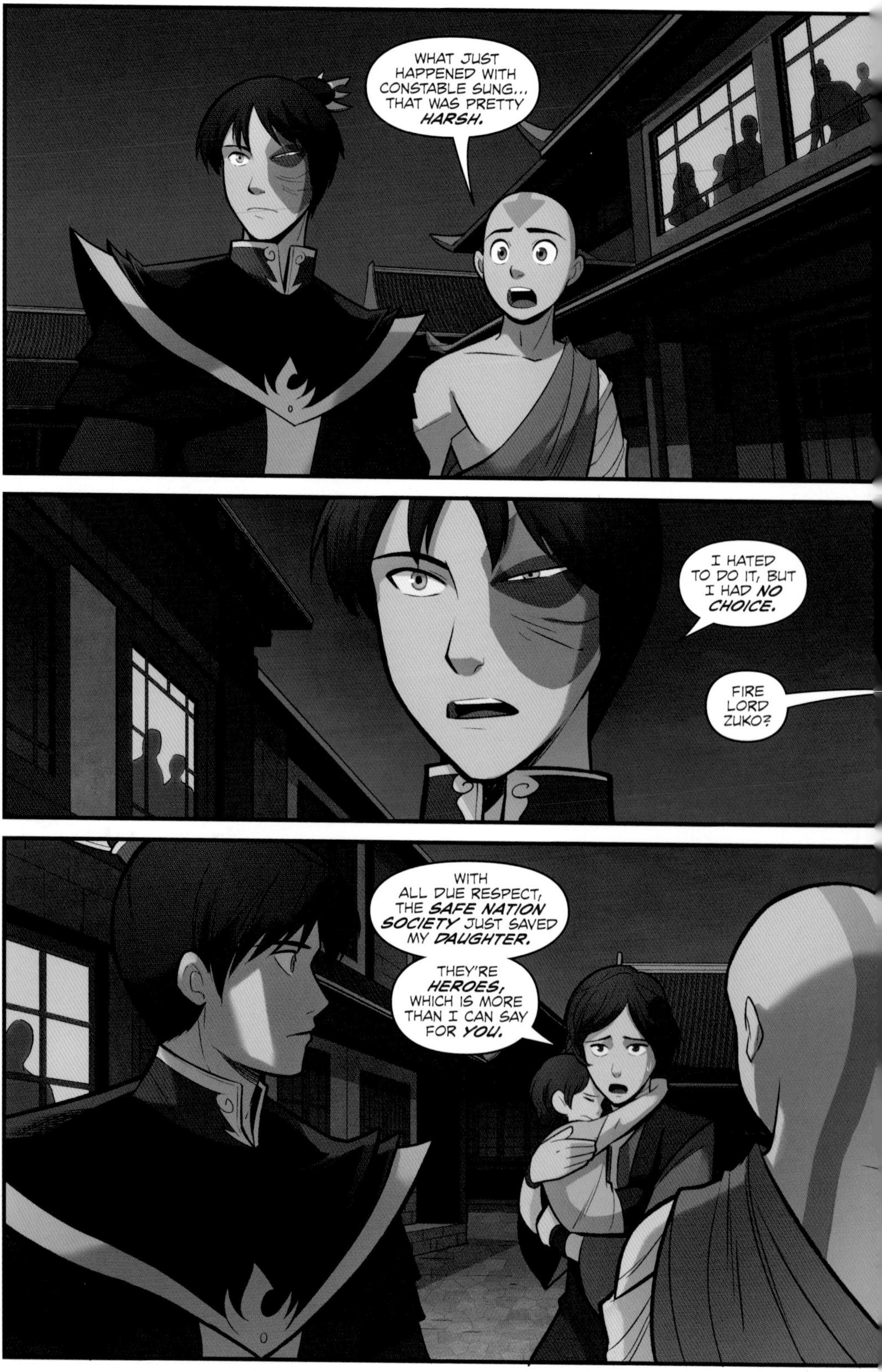
WHAT JUST HAPPENED WITH CONSTABLE SUNG... THAT WAS PRETTY *HARSH.*
I HATED TO DO IT, BUT I HAD *NO CHOICE.*
FIRE LORD ZUKO?
WITH ALL DUE RESPECT, THE *SAFE NATION SOCIETY* JUST SAVED MY *DAUGHTER.*
THEY'RE *HEROES,* WHICH IS MORE THAN I CAN SAY FOR *YOU.*

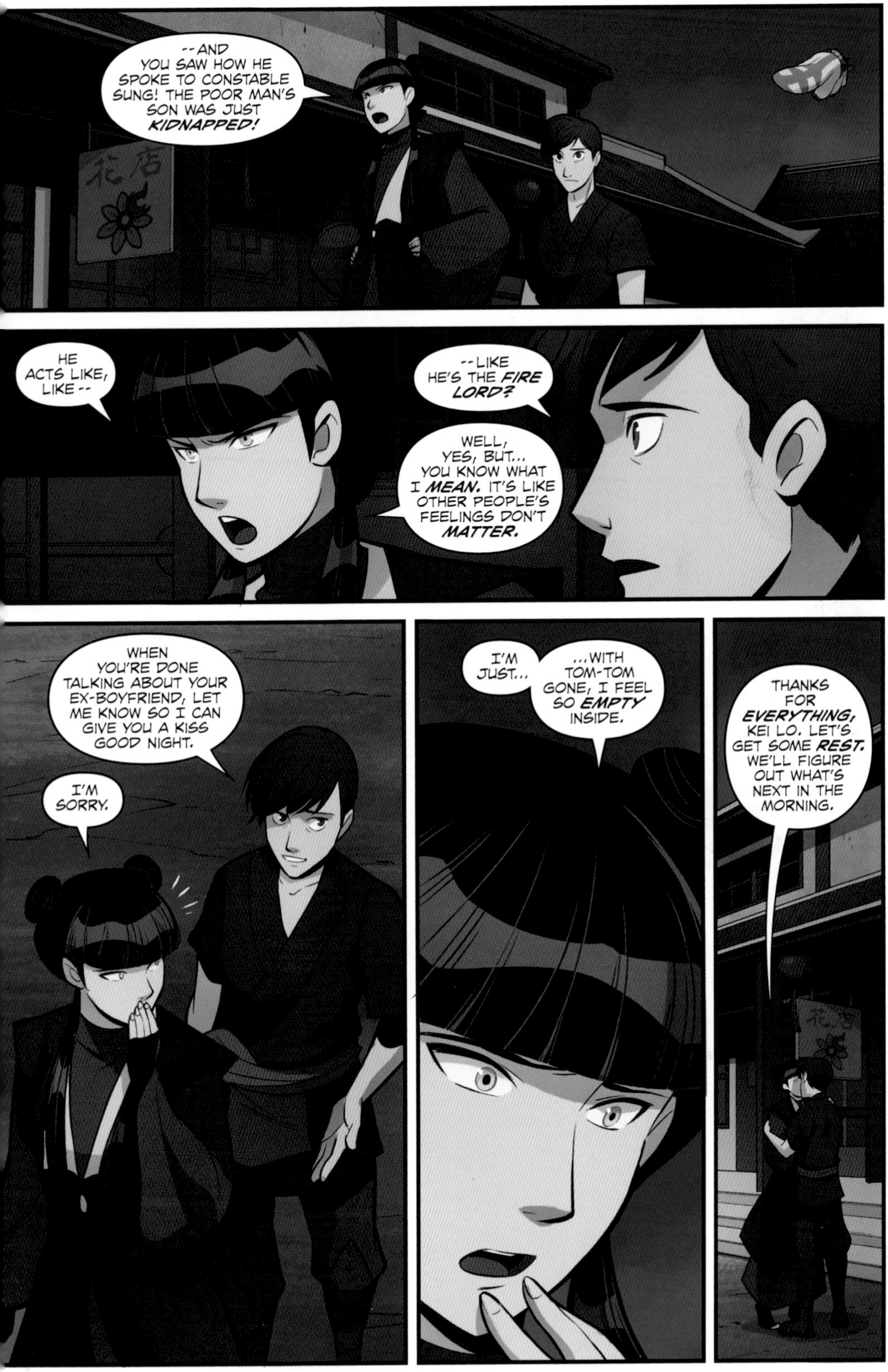
--AND YOU SAW HOW HE SPOKE TO CONSTABLE SUNG! THE POOR MAN'S SON WAS JUST KIDNAPPED!
HE ACTS LIKE, LIKE--
--LIKE HE'S THE FIRE LORD?
WELL, YES, BUT... YOU KNOW WHAT I MEAN. IT'S LIKE OTHER PEOPLE'S FEELINGS DON'T MATTER.
WHEN YOU'RE DONE TALKING ABOUT YOUR EX-BOYFRIEND, LET ME KNOW SO I CAN GIVE YOU A KISS GOOD NIGHT.
I'M SORRY.
I'M JUST...
...WITH TOM-TOM GONE, I FEEL SO EMPTY INSIDE.
THANKS FOR EVERYTHING, KEI LO. LET'S GET SOME REST. WE'LL FIGURE OUT WHAT'S NEXT IN THE MORNING.

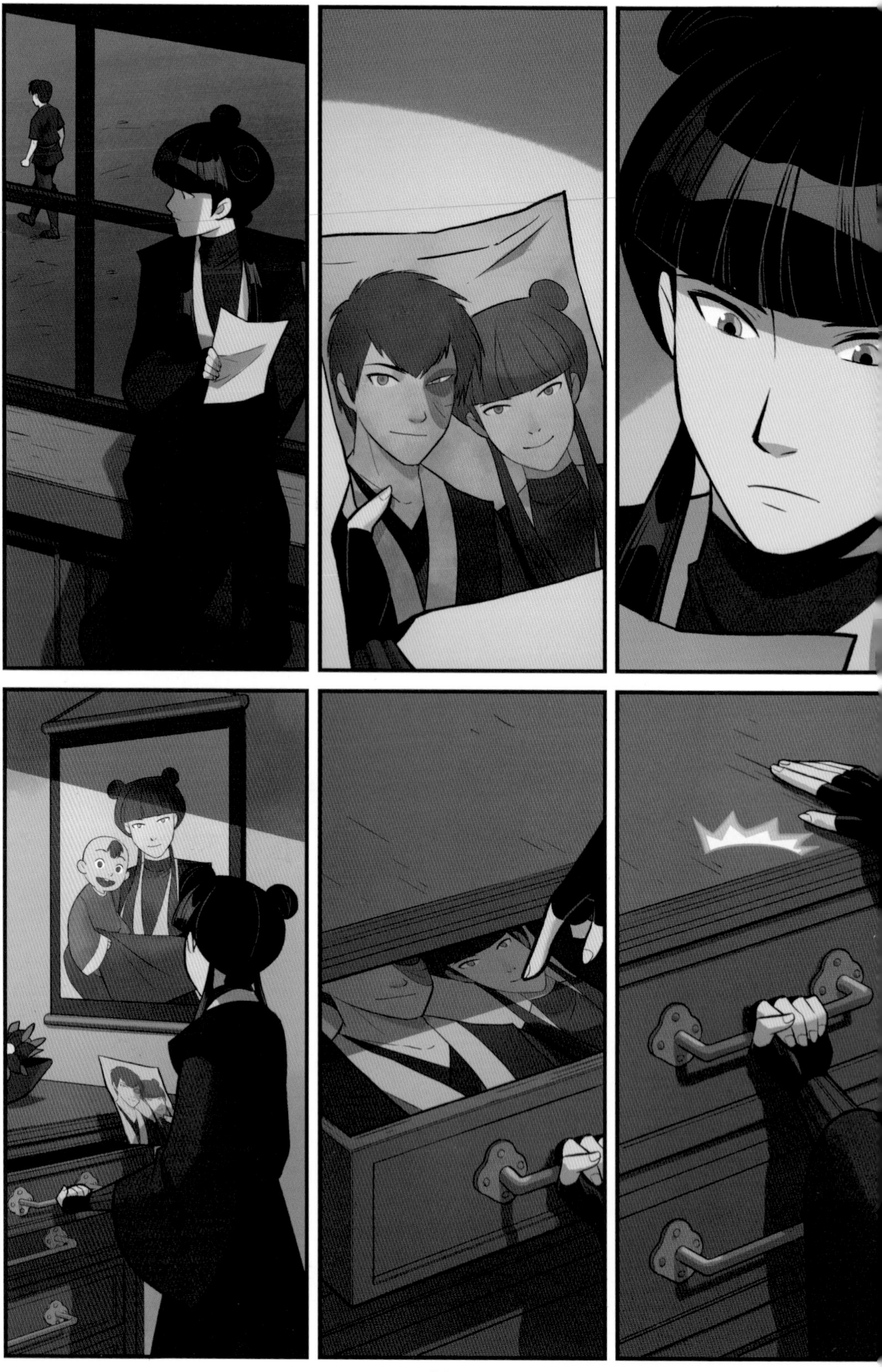

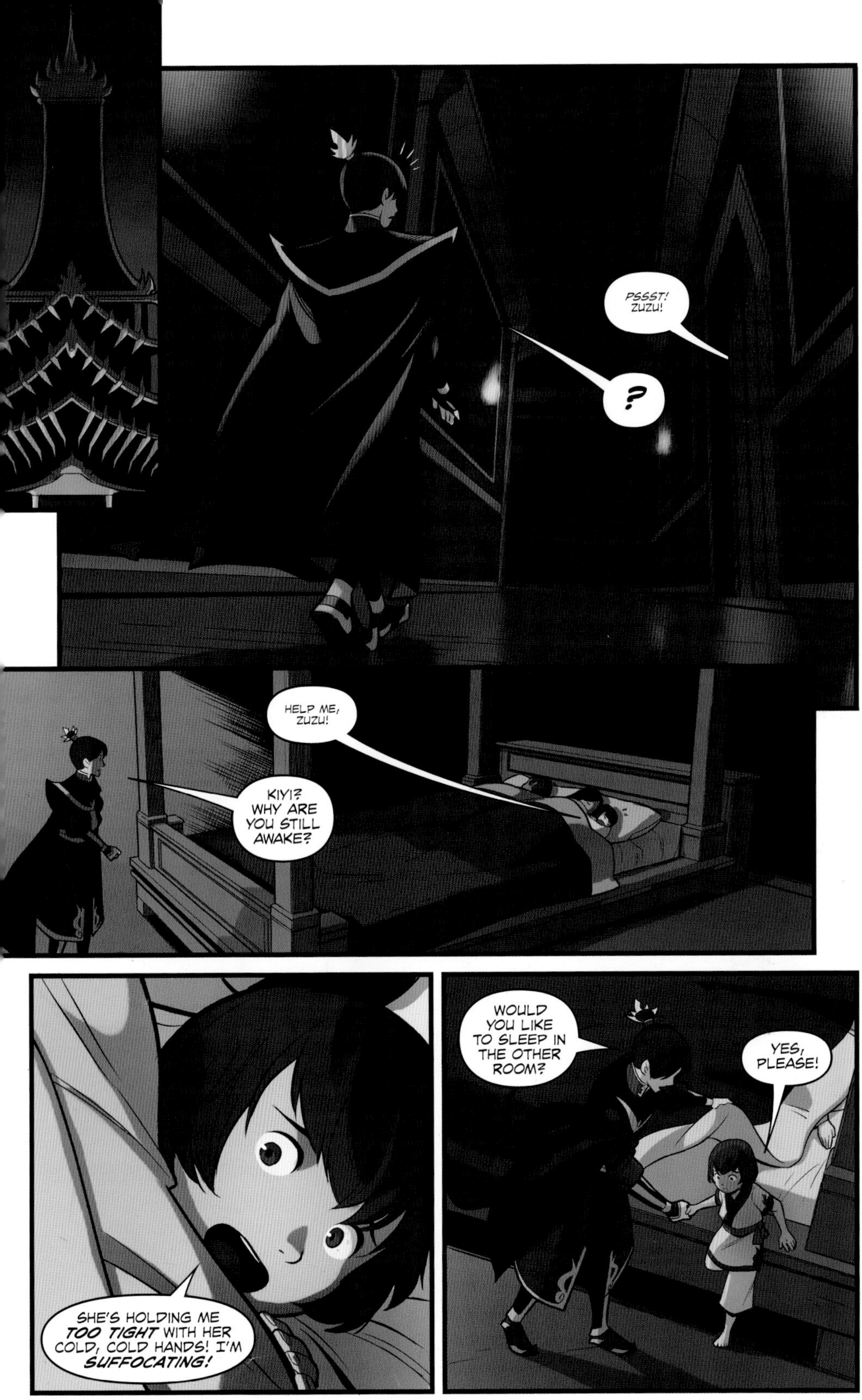
PSSST! ZUZU!
?
HELP ME, ZUZU!
KIYI? WHY ARE YOU STILL AWAKE?
SHE'S HOLDING ME TOO TIGHT WITH HER COLD, COLD HANDS! I'M SUFFOCATING!
WOULD YOU LIKE TO SLEEP IN THE OTHER ROOM?
YES, PLEASE!

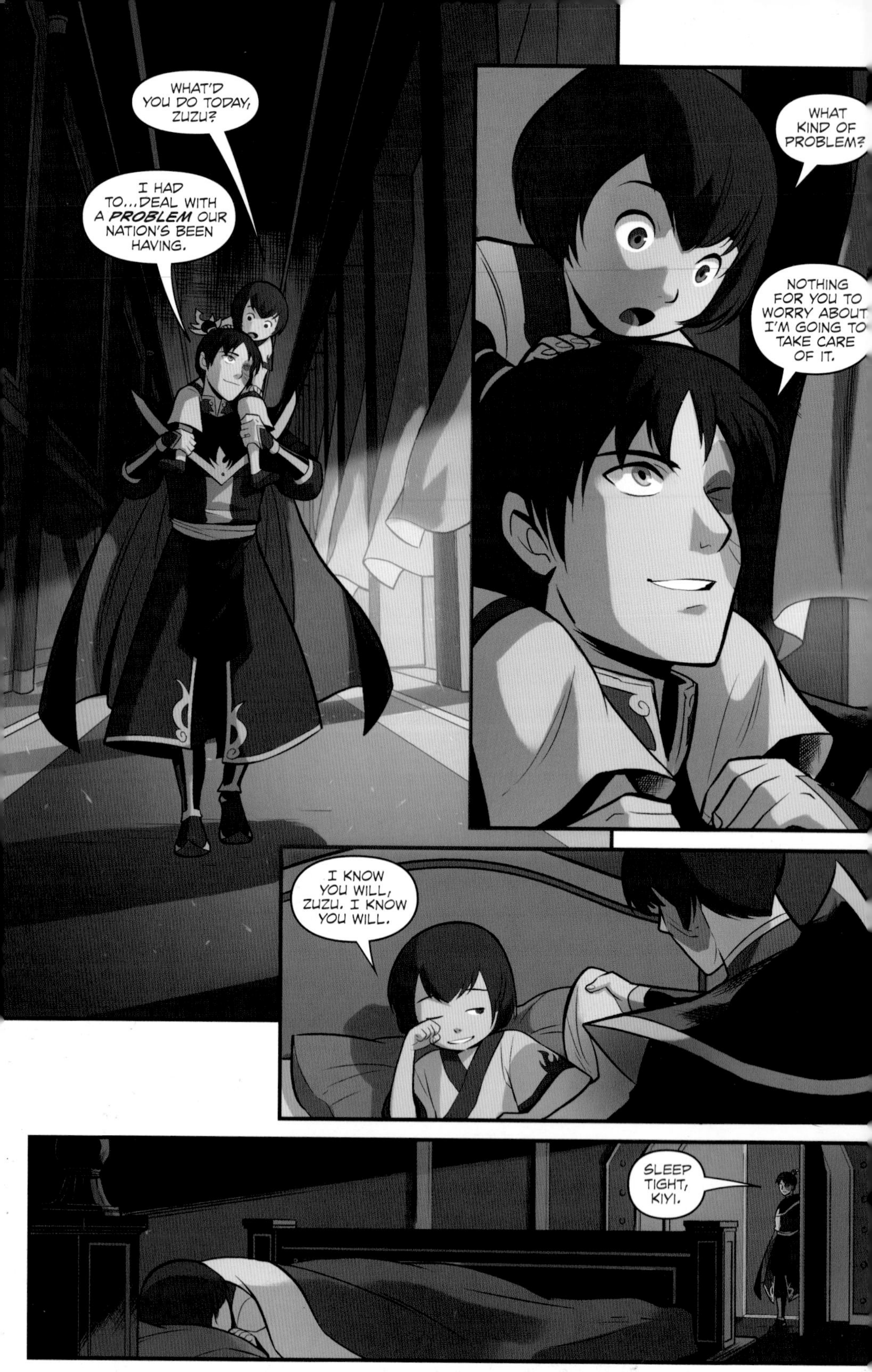
WHAT'D YOU DO TODAY, ZUZU?
I HAD TO...DEAL WITH A PROBLEM OUR NATION'S BEEN HAVING.
WHAT KIND OF PROBLEM?
NOTHING FOR YOU TO WORRY ABOUT. I'M GOING TO TAKE CARE OF IT.
I KNOW YOU WILL, ZUZU. I KNOW YOU WILL.
SLEEP TIGHT, KIYI.

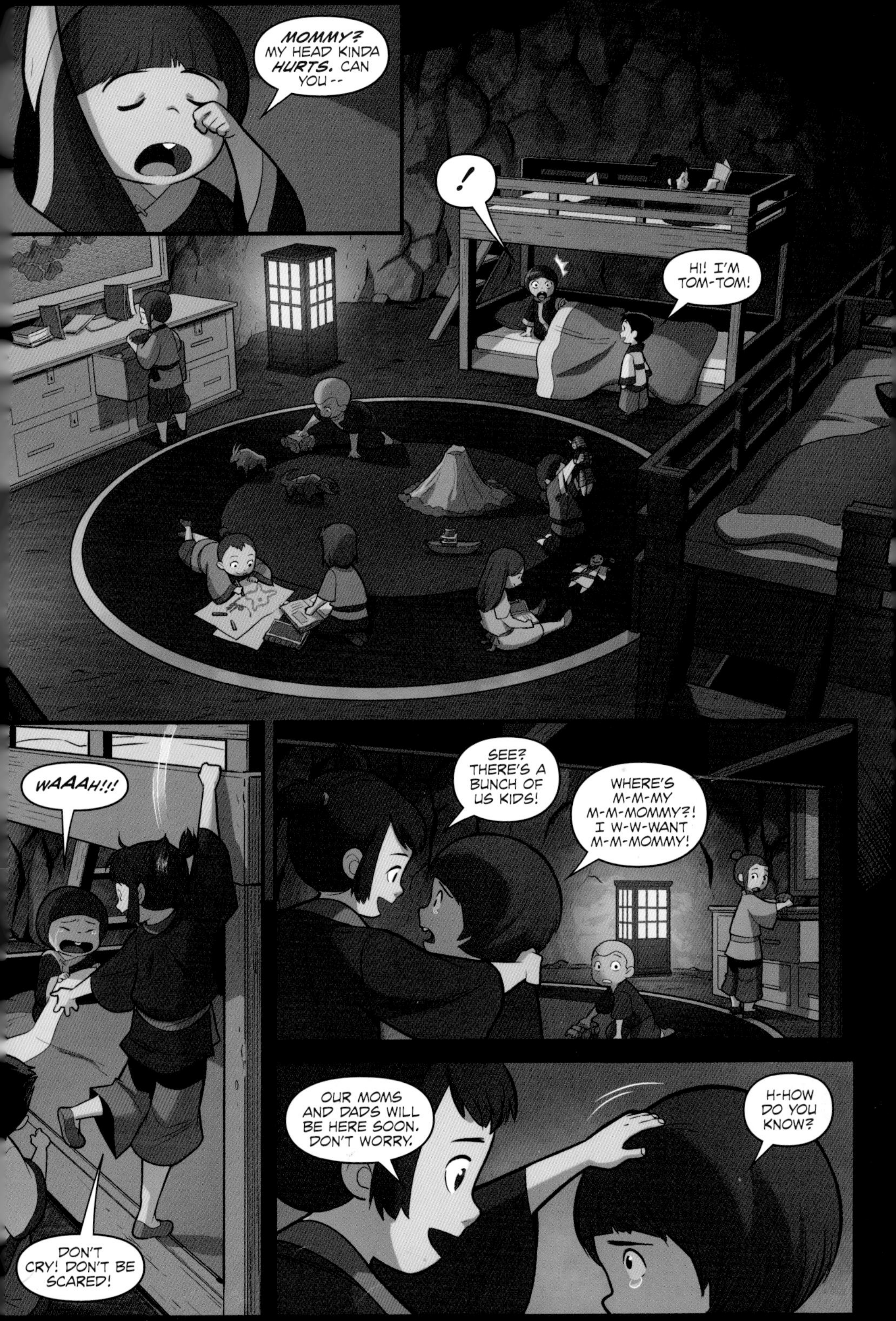
MOMMY? MY HEAD KINDA HURTS. CAN YOU --
!
HI! I'M TOM-TOM!
WAAAH!!!
DON'T CRY! DON'T BE SCARED!
SEE? THERE'S A BUNCH OF US KIDS!
WHERE'S M-M-MY M-M-MOMMY?! I W-W-WANT M-M-MOMMY!
OUR MOMS AND DADS WILL BE HERE SOON. DON'T WORRY.
H-HOW DO YOU KNOW?

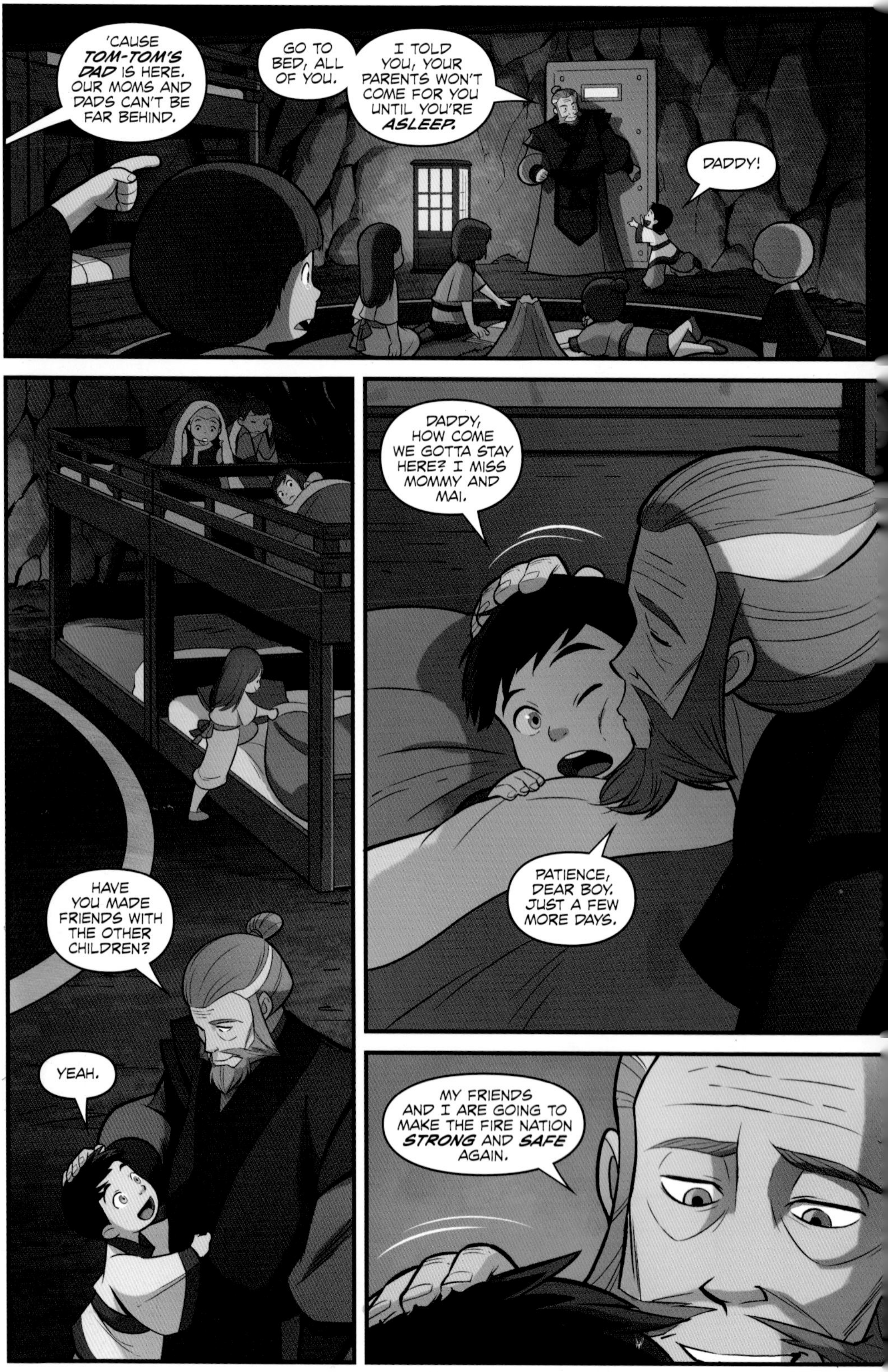
'CAUSE TOM-TOM'S DAD IS HERE. OUR MOMS AND DADS CAN'T BE FAR BEHIND.
GO TO BED, ALL OF YOU.
I TOLD YOU, YOUR PARENTS WON'T COME FOR YOU UNTIL YOU'RE ASLEEP.
DADDY!
HAVE YOU MADE FRIENDS WITH THE OTHER CHILDREN?
YEAH.
DADDY, HOW COME WE GOTTA STAY HERE? I MISS MOMMY AND MAI.
PATIENCE, DEAR BOY. JUST A FEW MORE DAYS.
MY FRIENDS AND I ARE GOING TO MAKE THE FIRE NATION STRONG AND SAFE AGAIN.

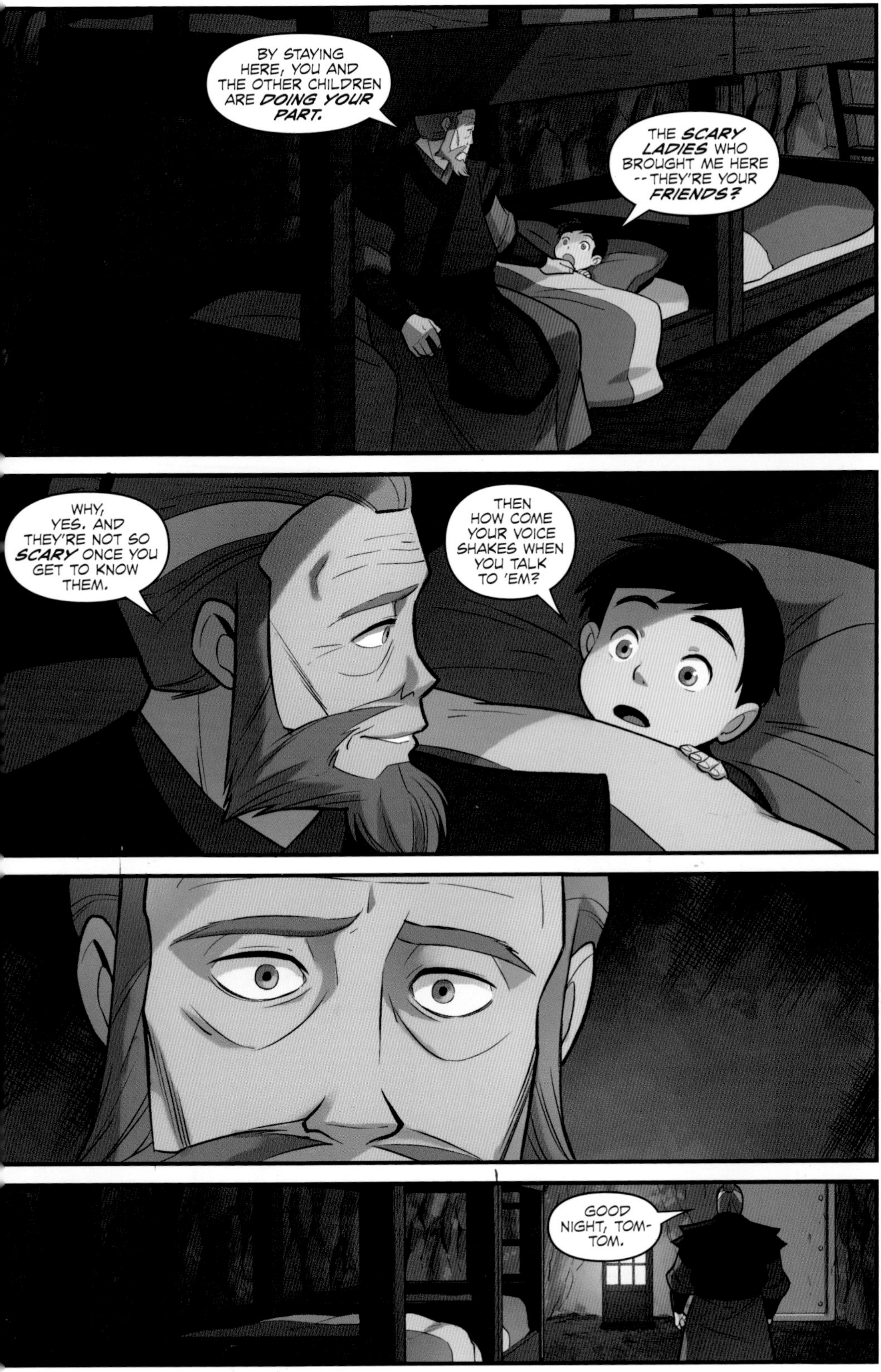
BY STAYING HERE, YOU AND THE OTHER CHILDREN ARE **DOING YOUR PART.**
THE **SCARY LADIES** WHO BROUGHT ME HERE --THEY'RE YOUR **FRIENDS?**
WHY, YES. AND THEY'RE NOT SO **SCARY** ONCE YOU GET TO KNOW THEM.
THEN HOW COME YOUR VOICE SHAKES WHEN YOU TALK TO 'EM?
GOOD NIGHT, TOM-TOM.

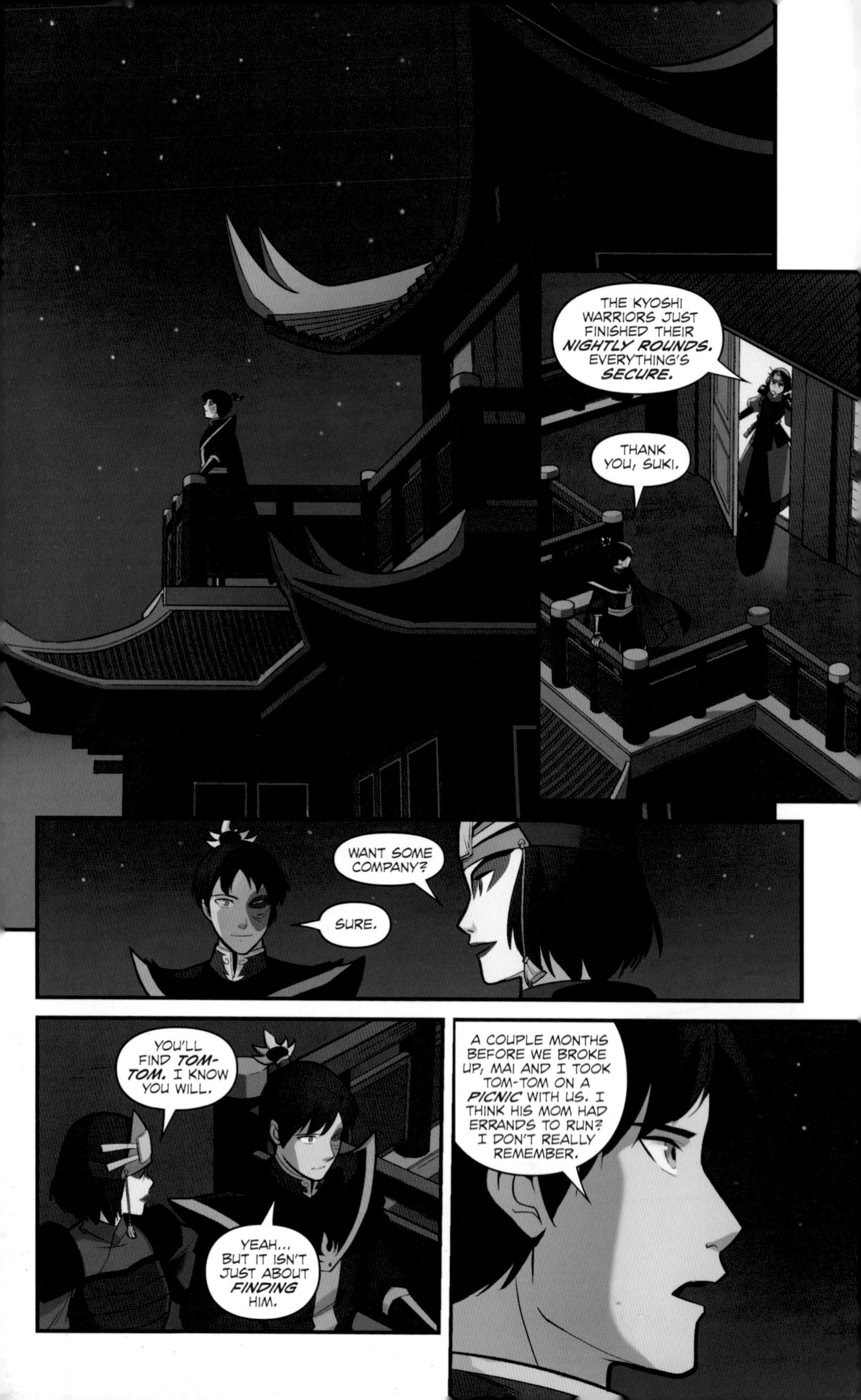
THE KYOSHI WARRIORS JUST FINISHED THEIR NIGHTLY ROUNDS. EVERYTHING'S SECURE.
THANK YOU, SUKI.
WANT SOME COMPANY?
SURE.
YOU'LL FIND TOM-TOM. I KNOW YOU WILL.
YEAH... BUT IT ISN'T JUST ABOUT FINDING HIM.
A COUPLE MONTHS BEFORE WE BROKE UP, MAI AND I TOOK TOM-TOM ON A PICNIC WITH US. I THINK HIS MOM HAD ERRANDS TO RUN? I DON'T REALLY REMEMBER.

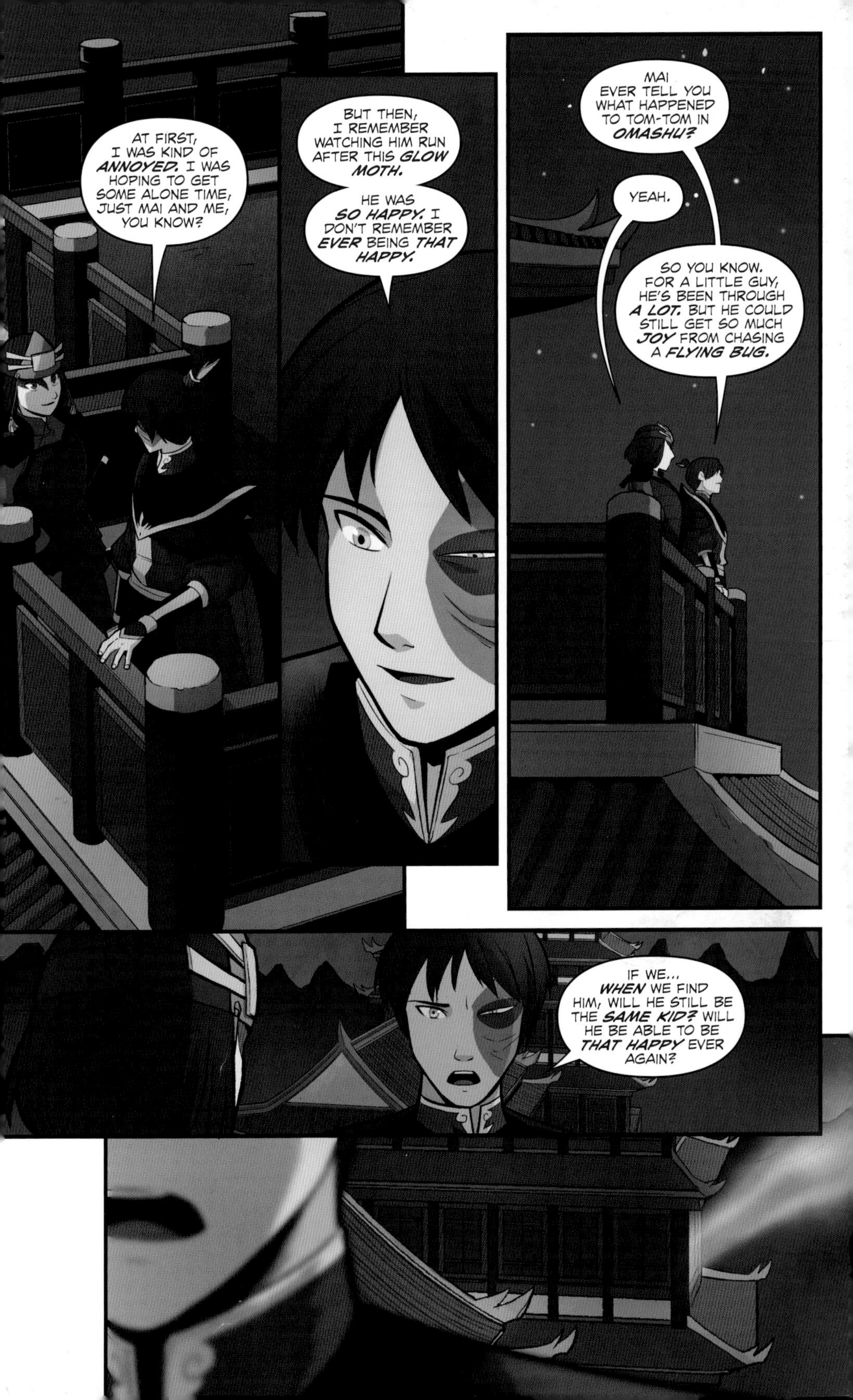
AT FIRST, I WAS KIND OF ANNOYED. I WAS HOPING TO GET SOME ALONE TIME, JUST MAI AND ME, YOU KNOW?
BUT THEN, I REMEMBER WATCHING HIM RUN AFTER THIS GLOW MOTH.
HE WAS SO HAPPY. I DON'T REMEMBER EVER BEING THAT HAPPY.
MAI EVER TELL YOU WHAT HAPPENED TO TOM-TOM IN OMASHU?
YEAH.
SO YOU KNOW. FOR A LITTLE GUY, HE'S BEEN THROUGH A LOT. BUT HE COULD STILL GET SO MUCH JOY FROM CHASING A FLYING BUG.
IF WE... WHEN WE FIND HIM, WILL HE STILL BE THE SAME KID? WILL HE BE ABLE TO BE THAT HAPPY EVER AGAIN?

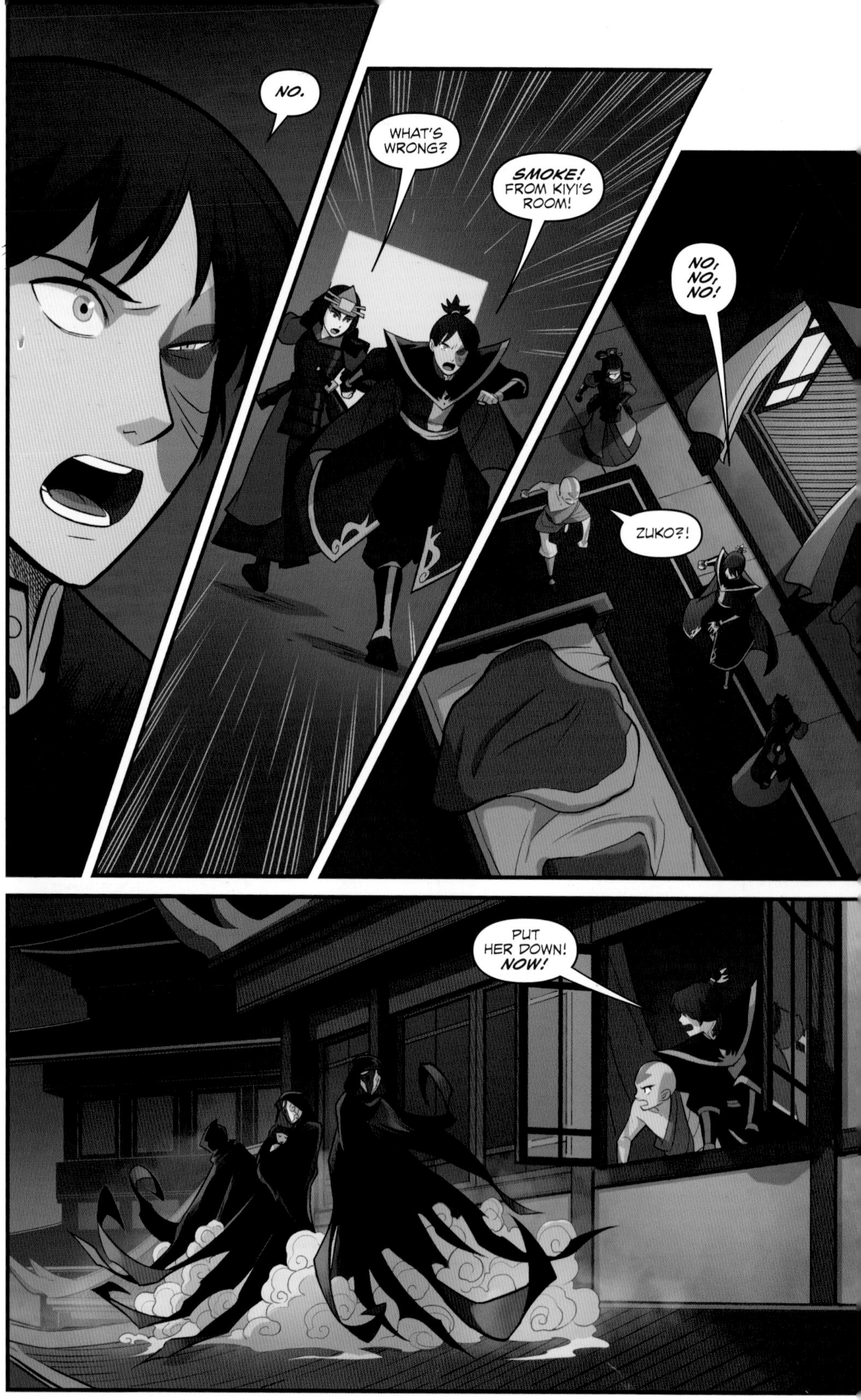
NO.
WHAT'S WRONG?
SMOKE! FROM KIYI'S ROOM!
NO, NO, NO!
ZUKO?!
PUT HER DOWN! NOW!

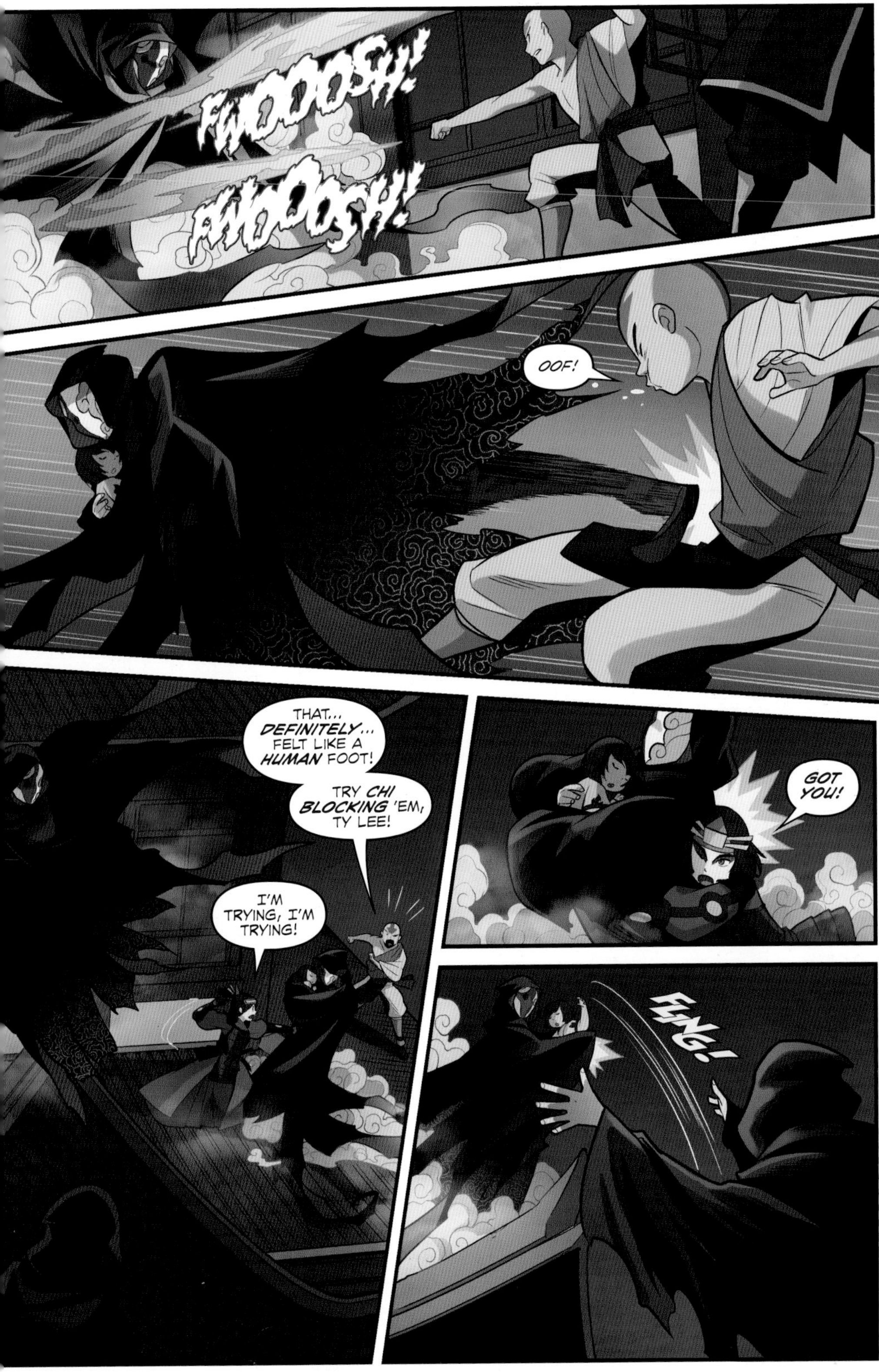
FWOOOSH!
FWOOOSH!
OOF!
THAT... DEFINITELY... FELT LIKE A HUMAN FOOT!
TRY CHI BLOCKING 'EM, TY LEE!
I'M TRYING, I'M TRYING!
GOT YOU!
FLING!

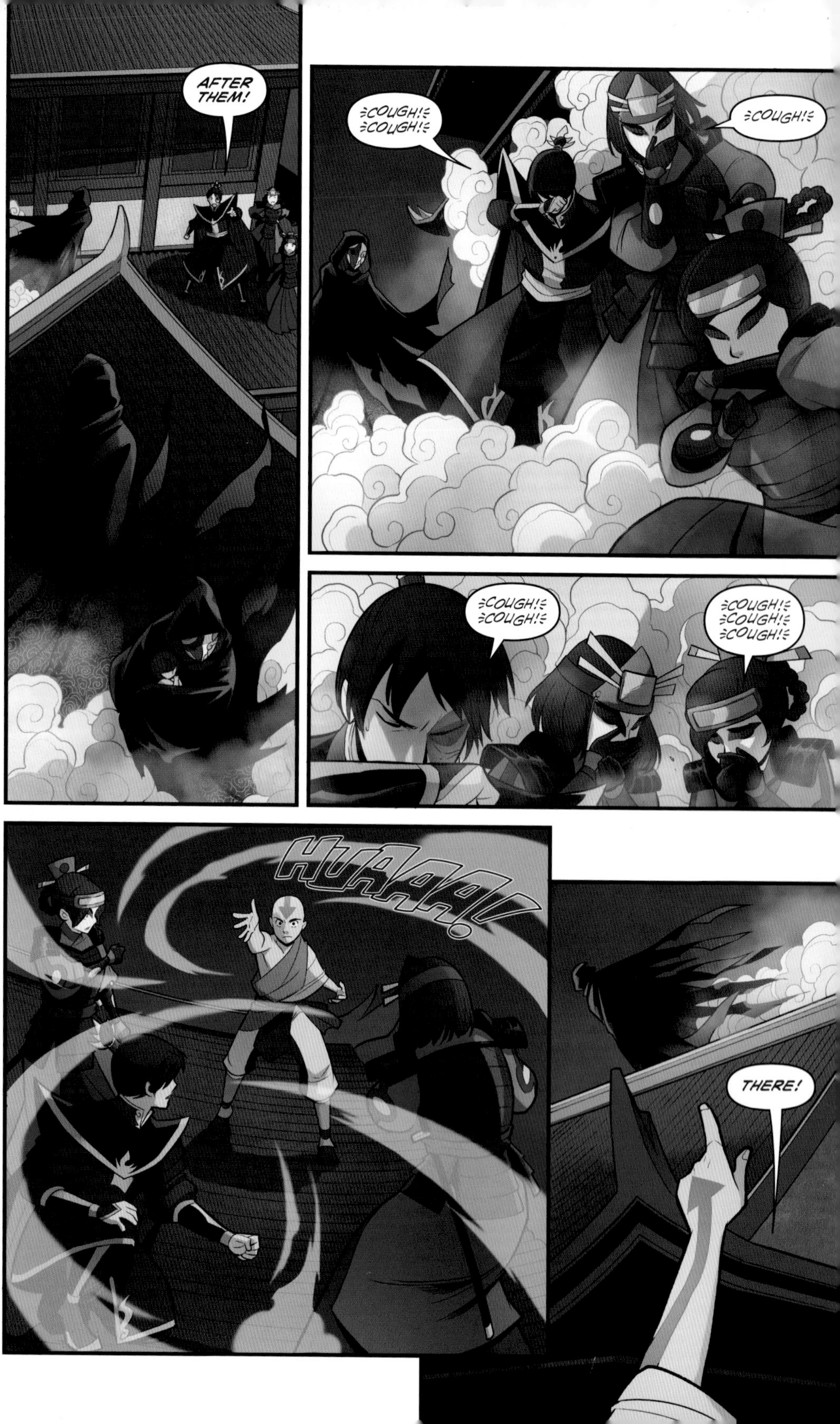

AFTER THEM!
COUGH! COUGH!
COUGH!
COUGH! COUGH!
COUGH! COUGH! COUGH!
HUAAAA!
THERE!

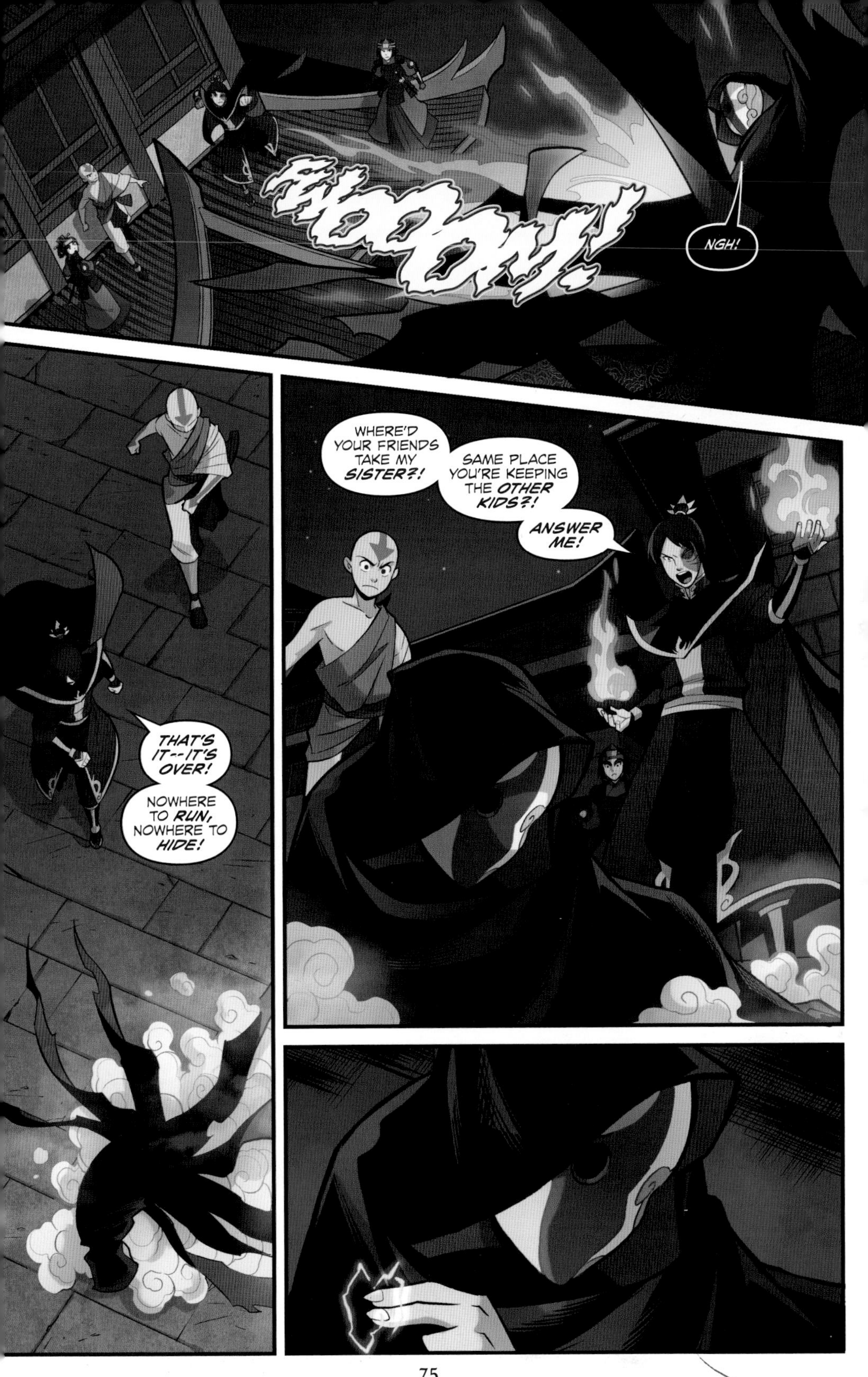
FWOOOM!
NGH!
THAT'S IT--IT'S OVER!
NOWHERE TO RUN, NOWHERE TO HIDE!
WHERE'D YOUR FRIENDS TAKE MY SISTER?!
SAME PLACE YOU'RE KEEPING THE OTHER KIDS?!
ANSWER ME!

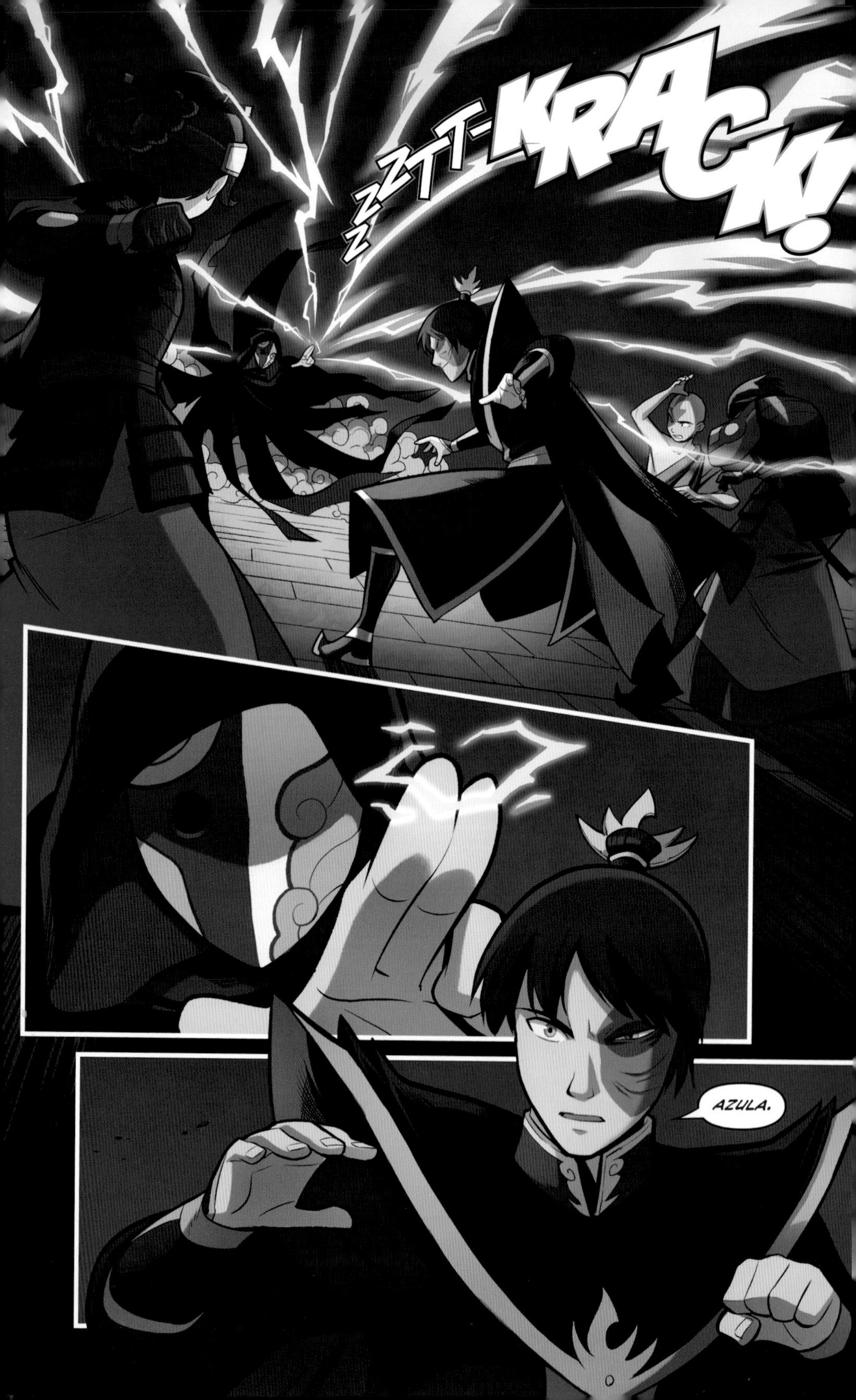
ZZZZTT-KRACK!
AZULA.

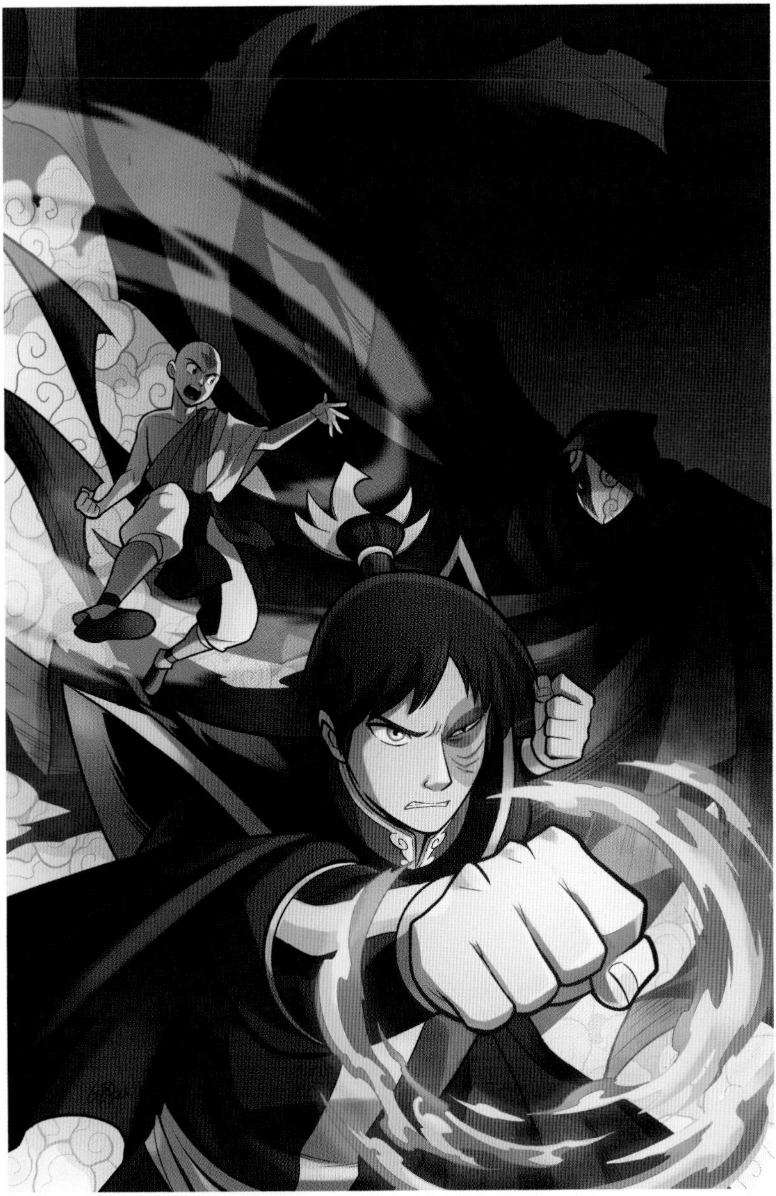

COMING IN MARCH

Zuko fights for the future of the Fire Nation in . . .

SMOKE AND SHADOW • PART THREE

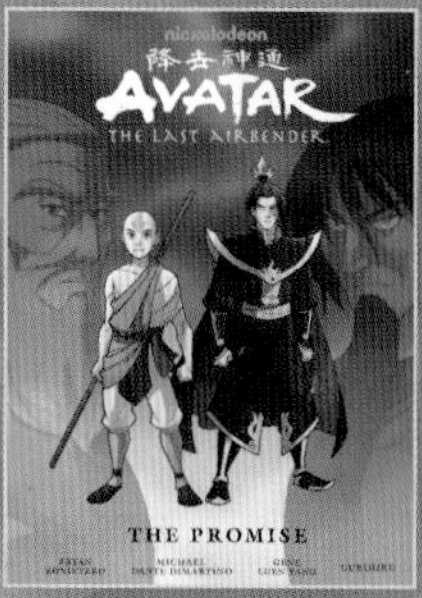
nickelodeon
AVATAR
THE LAST AIRBENDER
THE PROMISE

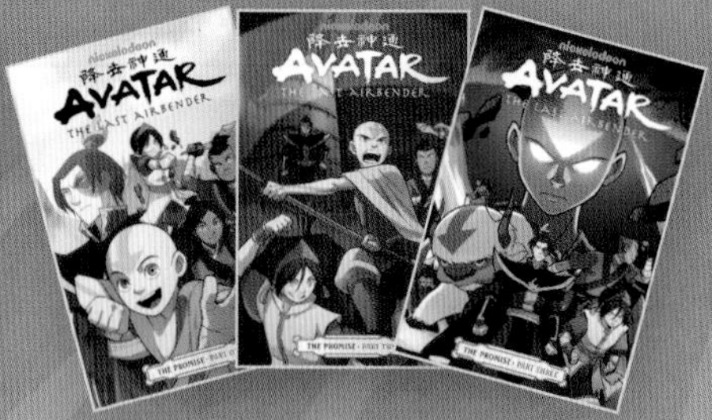

Avatar: The Last Airbender—The Promise Library Edition
978-1-61655-074-5 $39.99

Avatar: The Last Airbender—The Promise Part 1
978-1-59582-811-8 $10.99

Avatar: The Last Airbender—The Promise Part 2
978-1-59582-875-0 $10.99

Avatar: The Last Airbender—The Promise Part 3
978-1-59582-941-2 $10.99

Avatar: The Last Airbender—The Search Library Edition
978-1-61655-226-8 $39.99

Avatar: The Last Airbender—The Search Part 1
978-1-61655-054-7 $10.99

Avatar: The Last Airbender—The Search Part 2
978-1-61655-190-2 $10.99

Avatar: The Last Airbender—The Search Part 3
978-1-61655-184-1 $10.99

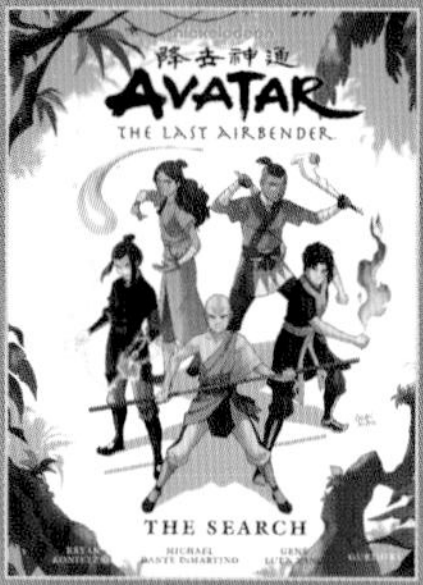
AVATAR
THE LAST AIRBENDER
THE SEARCH

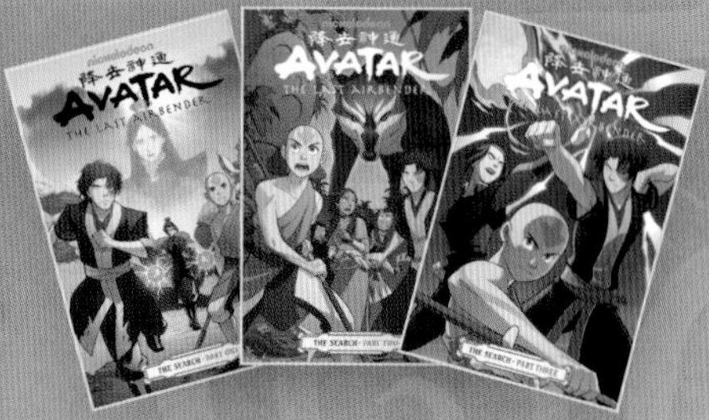

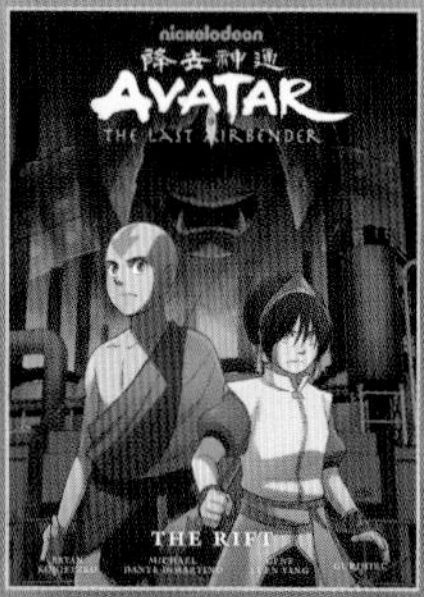
nickelodeon
AVATAR
THE LAST AIRBENDER
THE RIFT

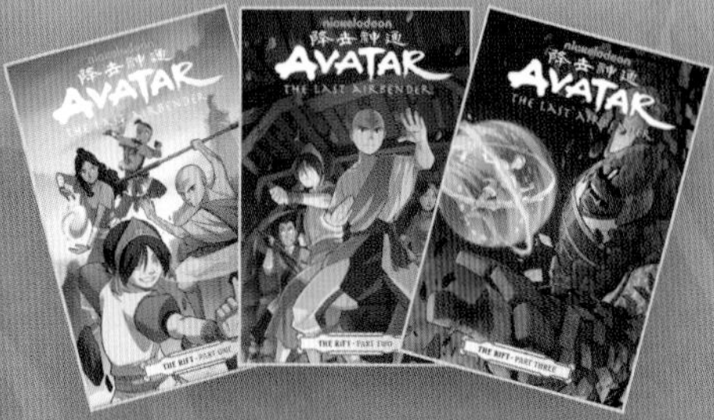

Avatar: The Last Airbender—The Rift Library Edition
978-1-61655-550-4 $39.99

Avatar: The Last Airbender—The Rift Part 1
978-1-61655-295-4 $10.99

Avatar: The Last Airbender—The Rift Part 2
978-1-61655-296-1 $10.99

Avatar: The Last Airbender—The Rift Part 3
978-1-61655-297-8 $10.99

Avatar: The Last Airbender—Smoke and Shadow Library Edition
978-1-50670-013-7 $39.99

Avatar: The Last Airbender—Smoke and Shadow Part 1
978-1-61655-761-4 $10.99

Avatar: The Last Airbender—Smoke and Shadow Part 2
978-1-61655-790-4 $10.99

Avatar: The Last Airbender—Smoke and Shadow Part 3
978-1-61655-838-3 $10.99

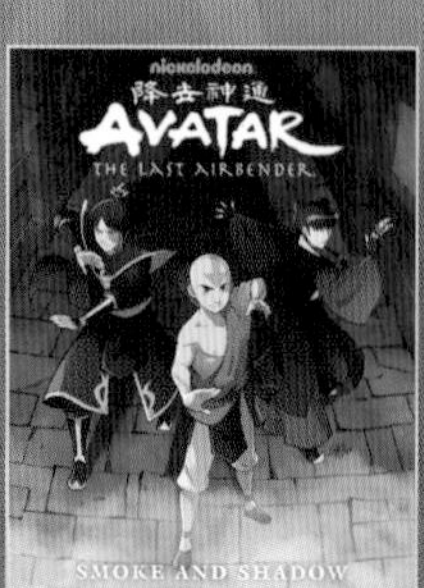
nickelodeon
AVATAR
THE LAST AIRBENDER
SMOKE AND SHADOW

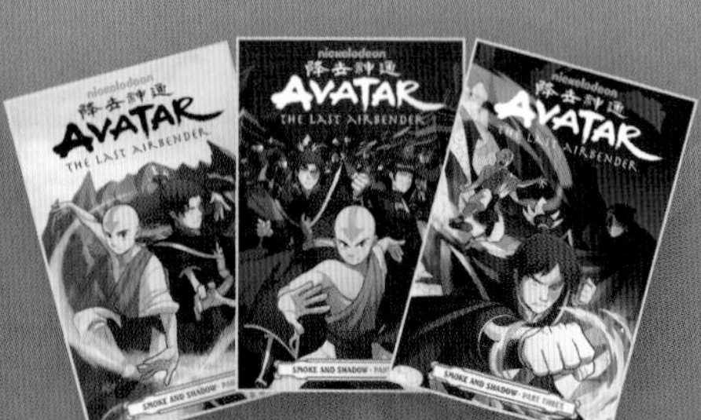

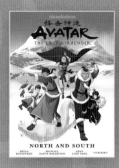

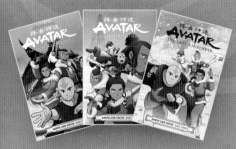

nickelodeon
AVATAR
THE LAST AIRBENDER
NORTH AND SOUTH
BRYAN KONIETZKO
MICHAEL DANTE DiMARTINO
GENE LUEN YANG
GURIHIRU

AVATAR
AVATAR
AVATAR

Avatar: The Last Airbender—North And South Library Edition
978-1-50670-195-0 $39.99

Avatar: The Last Airbender—North and South Part 1
978-1-50670-022-9 $10.99

Avatar: The Last Airbender—North and South Part 2
978-1-50670-129-5 $10.99

Avatar: The Last Airbender—North and South Part 3
978-1-50670-130-1 $10.99

nickelodeon

降去神通

AVATAR

THE LAST AIRBENDER

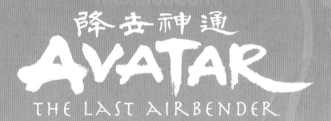

BE PART OF THE INCREDIBLE JOURNEY!

Check out the best-selling graphic novels and recapture the magic!

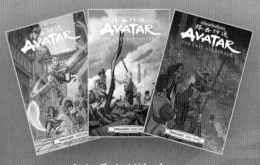

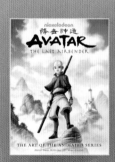

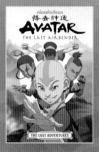

nickelodeon
AVATAR
THE LAST AIRBENDER
THE ART OF THE ANIMATED SERIES

AVATAR
AVATAR
THE LAST AIRBENDER
AVATAR
THE LAST AIRBENDER
IMBALANCE · PART ONE
IMBALANCE · PART TWO
IMBALANCE · PART THREE

nickelodeon
AVATAR
THE LAST AIRBENDER
THE LOST ADVENTURES

Avatar: The Last Airbender—Imbalance Part 1
978-1-50670-489-0 $10.99

Avatar: The Last Airbender—The Art of the Animated Series
978-1-59582-504-9 $34.99

Avatar: The Last Airbender—Imbalance Part 2
978-1-50670-652-8 $10.99

Avatar: The Last Airbender—Imbalance Part 3
978-1-50670-813-3 $10.99

Avatar: The Last Airbender—The Lost Adventures
978-1-59582-748-7 $14.99

AVAILABLE AT YOUR LOCAL COMICS SHOP OR BOOKSTORE! To find a comics shop in your area, visit comicshoplocator.com. For more information or to order direct visit DarkHorse.com or call 1-800-862-0052

DARK HORSE BOOKS

The Legend of Korra:
Turf Wars Library Edition
978-1-50670-202-5 $39.99

The Legend of Korra:
Turf Wars Part One
978-1-50670-014-1 $10.99

The Legend of Korra:
Turf Wars Part Two
978-1-50670-040-3 $10.99

The Legend of Korra:
Turf Wars Part Three
978-1-50670-185-1 $10.99

JOIN AVATAR KORRA AND TEAM AVATAR
IN A NEW AGE OF ADVENTURE!

The Legend of Korra:
The Animated Series
Book One: Air
978-1-61655-168-1 $34.99

Book Two: Spirits
978-1-61655-462-0 $34.99

Book Three: Change
978-1-61655-565-8 $34.99

Book Four: Balance
978-1-61655-687-7 $34.99

The Legend of Korra:
Ruins of the Empire Part One
978-1-50670-894-2 $10.99

The Legend of Korra:
Ruins of the Empire Part Two
978-1-50670-895-9 $10.99

AVAILABLE AT YOUR LOCAL COMICS SHOP OR BOOKSTORE! To find a comics shop in your area, visit
comicshoplocator.com. For more information or to order direct visit DarkHorse.com or email: mailorder@darkhorse.com

© Viacom International Inc. All Rights Reserved. The Legend of Korra and all related titles, logos and characters are trademarks of Viacom International Inc.
Dark Horse Books® and the Dark Horse logo are registered trademarks of Dark Horse Comics LLC. All Rights Reserved (BL 6011)